Physical Fitness: A Way of Life

6th Edition

Alan E. Mikesky, Ph.D.

Kay N. Mikesky, M.S.

Bud Getchell, Ph.D.

Library of Congress Cataloging in Publication Data:

Mikesky, Alan E., 1955

Physical Fitness: A Way of Life, 6th Edition

Library of Congress Control Number: 2006931582

ISBN: 0976930331

Cover Design: Gary Schmitt

Publisher: I. L. Cooper

Printed in the United States of America. Published by Cooper Publishing Group, LLC, P.O. Box 1129, Traverse City, MI 49685.

www.cooperpublishinggroup.com

10 9 8 7 6 5 4 3 2 1

The Publisher and Author disclaim responsibility for any adverse effects or consequences from the misapplication or injudicious use of the information contained within this text.

Table of Contents

Preface

The sixth edition of Physical Fitness: A Way of Life continues the text's thirty one year tradition of taking a positive, realistic, and fun approach to teaching the basics of how to design and implement your personalized exercise program. Regardless of your past experiences with sports or exercise, you'll find information in this book to be easy to understand and hopefully enjoyable to read. It is not a book filled with heart disease statistics, anatomical terms or physiologic details on how a muscle fiber contracts. Such in-depth information is not necessary to take action and begin adopting strategies that enable you to experience the good feeling associated with being active and in shape.

This text is geared toward the fitness enthusiast and would make an excellent supplement for high school or college-level elective exercise classes. The book does not have to be read in any particular sequence, and depending on the focus of the class, only the pertinent chapters need to be referred to. Also, in the Appendix training logs have been included so that this text serves both an informational and record keeping role in the class. As mentioned previously the reader does not need a background in exercise science to understand the information contained within the pages of this book. Chapter 1 helps the reader to understand the concept of wellness, its association with health, and the role physical fitness plays in achieving both. Chapter 2 addresses some of the misconceptions that are commonly held regarding exercise. Testing and assessment of the various health related components of physical fitness are discussed in Chapter 3. Chapter 4 explains the four basic training principles that must be understood in order to put together a safe and effective exercise program. Chapters 5 through 9 cover the different health-related components of physical fitness and provide details on the "how to" aspects of putting a program together that improves each component. Chapter 10 is the final chapter and discusses strategies on how to make exercise a way of life. Finally, the Appendix includes a form for plotting changes in physical fitness and over twenty pages of aerobic and resistance training logs for keeping track of workouts.

Several pedagogical strategies have been implemented in this new edition. The introduction of each chapter includes a series of questions that the reader should try to answer before reading further. This does several things: it focuses attention on the topics to be covered in the chapter; it primes the reader's thoughts about the topics to be covered by having them try to answer the questions with what they currently know, or at least think they know, about the topics; and it helps to identify and correct any misconceptions they may have about exercise. Additionally, major headings and sub-headings within the chapters are worded as questions to foster purposeful reading. In other words, students are "directed" to read further with the intent of answering the heading or subheading questions. The goal is to prevent "hollow reading" in which a person reads the words on the pages but without any perspective as to why they are reading. In addition, key words are bolded in the text and defined in easy to find sidebars. Finally, "A Way of Life Boxes" are found throughout the chapters to highlight key points, give training tips and provide inspiration. The primary objective is to inform the reader so they can adopt an active lifestyle.

Let's not kid ourselves: it takes effort to get and stay in shape. There is no magic program or easy way to be physically fit. However, fitness exercise does not have to be punishing exercise. You need to challenge your body, but the challenge should be within your own capabilities, which means that almost anyone can safely participate in an exercise program. Reading through this book will give you what you need to successfully make exercise a way of life.

Health, Wellness, and Physical Fitness

This is a book about you. It is a book about developing and maintaining a healthy level of physical fitness. While most people know that regular exercise combined with sound nutrition is good for their health, they simply do nothing about it. The biggest hurdle is finding the time. This book will teach you the basics of exercise and how to incorporate them into a busy daily schedule so that ultimately they become "a way of life".

This chapter introduces you to the concepts of health, wellness, and physical fitness. It discusses how they are related but not one in the same. Read the following questions and after each one formulate the answer in your mind. If you don't know the answer, then read the chapter with the intent of finding the answer. If you did answer the question, then read to make sure your answer is correct and not a misconception you have about health, wellness, or physical fitness.

- How do health, wellness, and physical fitness differ from one another?
- Why is living longer not necessarily better?
- What did the 1996 Surgeon General's Report state was a nationwide health concern? What is recommended by the updated guidelines to help alleviate this problem?
- What is it about today's lifestyle that fosters poor physical fitness?
- What does it mean when someone is said to be "physically fit"?
- What are the various components of physical fitness?

- What does it take to become healthier and more physically fit?

GOOD HEALTH: IS IT THE KEY TO LIVING LONGER OR BETTER?

According to Webster's Dictionary, the definition of **health** is "the condition of being sound in body, mind, or spirit". In other words,

> **HEALTH:**
> The general condition of one's physical, intellectual, social, emotional, occupational, environmental, and spiritual being.

it is more than just freedom from physical disease and/or pain. Health is multi-faceted and includes physical, intellectual, emotional, spiritual, occupational, environmental, and social components. **Wellness** is "optimal health" in

> **WELLNESS:**
> The state of health that results when physical, intellectual, spiritual, social, occupational, environmental, and emotional components are all at optimal levels.

which all seven components have reached their highest level. The opposite of wellness is death.

Figure 1.1 graphically demonstrates that health is a varying state with death and wellness at its extremes. This concept is known as the **Health Continuum**. Our level of health changes from day to day throughout life depending on the

> **HEALTH CONTINUUM:**
> A conceptual view of a person's state of health that spans from wellness (i.e. optimal health) to death.

state of each component. Due to sedentary lifestyles the physical health of many Americans lags behind the other components. Therefore, on the continuum these people are 'just getting by. It is generally agreed by fitness and health experts that regular exercise is essential to the pursuit of wellness.

Being physically fit does not guarantee you health but it can be the key to living a fuller life. The effort it takes for you to be physically fit can be a sound investment toward leading a happy, fulfilling life while decreasing your risk for disease. A question you might ask is, how much exercise do I need in order to realize some health benefits? Perhaps you are concerned only about living longer. Several epidemiological studies have investigated the relationship between physical fitness and death rates. After following large groups of men and women of varying fitness levels over many years, these studies have shown that the sedentary individuals who are least fit have death rates more than three times greater than those who are very active and most fit. Furthermore, findings from these studies also indicate that mortality

A WAY OF LIFE

Being physically fit does not guarantee you freedom from disease but it can definitely be the key to living a fuller life.

from heart disease, certain cancers, and other health-related causes can be attained using moderate intensity activity such as brisk walking. In other words, health benefits can be attained without performing high-intensity, strenuous, and/or painful physical exertion.

These studies suggest that moderate exercise seems to be adequate for helping you to

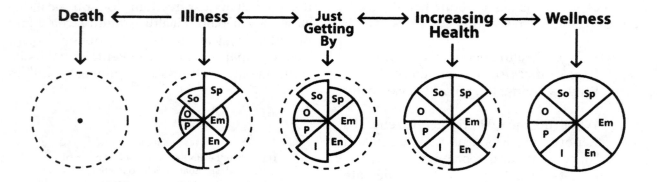

Figure 1.1: The Health Continuum: At the extremes of the continuum are death and wellness. Between the extremes are varying degrees of health based on the status of its seven components: So=Social, Sp=Spiritual, En=Environmental, O=Occupational, Em=Emotional, I=Intellectual, and P=Physical. The three depictions under the Health Continuum are graphic representations of the status of each component of health. The dashed circle represents the optimal level of each component. The graphic under "Just Getting By" is only one example of the many possible combinations at this point on the continuum. The key point is that some of the person's components of health are not at optimal.

live longer. But is living longer your only goal? How long is "longer"? A classic study by Paffenbarger and colleagues on Harvard graduates looked at the influence of exercise on longevity. Paffenbarger concluded that men who expended 2,000 calories a week exercising (i.e. the equivalent of working out 4 to 6 times) lived one to two years longer than sedentary individuals. It could easily be argued that exercising 4 to 5 days per week throughout your life is a lot of effort to increase your longevity a mere year or two.

The key here is to understand that it is not how long you live but whether you are capable of living life to its fullest. In other words, being healthy is more than just living longer. Being healthy is also about striving to live better. This is the main theme of this book. People exercise to maintain a good physical appearance, to have more energy to carry out everyday tasks, to sleep better, to be able to eat nutritious foods

A WAY OF LIFE

Being healthy is not just about how long you live but whether you are capable of living life to its fullest.

without worrying about weight gain, to improve their performance in a favorite sport or pastime, and most important, to enjoy the feeling of being physically fit and possessing good health. In short, being healthy will add years to your life and more importantly, life to your years.

WHAT'S THE DIFFERENCE BETWEEN HEALTH AND WELLNESS?

Recently health professionals have expressed health in terms of degrees. (see Figure 1.1.) The health continuum illustrates the broad scope of health from death (total absence of health) to the optimal level of health (wellness). How do you rate your health? Most people would answer, "Good," or "I'm fine." If you haven't been sick recently or been to a doctor, you most likely would say you are healthy.

In fact, most people feel that if they are able to carry out their everyday activities, then they are in good shape. In other words they are not sick. On the health continuum such people generally fall in the middle in the "just getting by" zone. They are not ill and may look well, but they may not be especially healthy either. High-level health means more than just getting by. It is more than being able to attend classes, play intramural sports one to two times a week, work at a regular job, and being active in social events. It means being physically active on a regular basis, eating properly, adhering to good sleep practices, and living life with enthusiasm and vigor. Granted, the health risks at the middle of the continuum are not fatal; however, living at a level of "just getting by" robs you of the type of life that wellness and physical fitness can afford you. In fact, some of the poor health behaviors associated with "just getting by" slowly cause changes in the body that become detrimental to good health in later life. More important, regardless of your age or present position, those who live in the neutral zone of the health continuum are not living up to their fullest potential. That's the point; what many people have come to accept as "good health" (i.e. just getting by) falls far short of what their health could "and should" be.

A WAY OF LIFE

What many people have come to accept as good health falls far short of what their health could—and should—be.

Recently, the United States Centers for Disease Control has promoted the theory that poor personal health behavior is the major reason for mortality. In other words, your personal lifestyle is a major determinant of early death (see Figure 1.2).

In 1996 at a White House press conference, a powerful message titled "The Surgeon General's Report on Physical Activity and Health" was made public. Its central message highlighted the importance of regular physical ac-

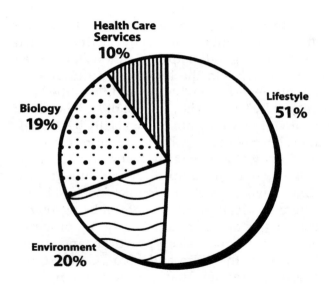

Figure 1.2: Major Factors in Mortality in the United States

tivity for improving and maintaining health and well being. The report was based on the most comprehensive review of the research literature dealing with physical inactivity and exercise and conclusively linked physical inactivity to increased risk for disease. In fact, the historical report labeled physical inactivity as a nationwide public health problem. As stated by then acting Surgeon General Audrey Manley, "...the report is more than a summary of the science, it is a national call to action" to reduce unnecessary health problems resulting from sedentary lifestyles. It was hoped that this report would help catalyze a new physical activity and fitness movement in the United States. Unfortunately the vast majority of Americans have yet to heed this advice.

Today, more than ever, assuring good health requires you to focus on such health-related behaviors as exercise and nutrition. For improvements in health we all need to look at changing the way we live and our personal health habits rather than continuing to rely on modern medicine to keep us well. Keep in

A WAY OF LIFE

Today, more than ever, we need to shift our approach to good health from one of treatment to one of prevention.

mind that health is a mix of factors; physical, intellectual, emotional, spiritual, social, environmental, and occupational. Even though you don't have total control over all the factors that constitute your health, you can take the responsibility for practicing smart, preventive health behaviors that will maximize the control you do have. When the first edition of this book was written, we proposed that regular physical activity (i.e. exercise) was a key component of good health. Twenty-five plus years later the research evidence unequivocally supports this view. Medical experts now realize that engaging in exercise on a regular basis is one of the keys to health and physical fitness.

A WAY OF LIFE

Medical experts now realize that engaging in exercise on a regular basis is key to health and physical fitness.

WHY IS EXERCISE CALLED THE "POSITIVE DO"?

When people think of health many times they associate it with a life full of "don'ts". In other words, "Don't eat that", "don't eat so much", "don't stay up late", etc. Rather than taking an all negative view on how to achieve better health how about thinking about what you can "do"? In other words, "do exercise." Exercise is good for you. It can be the "positive do" in your life that doesn't leave you with a sense of loss. Research has shown that people who start to exercise tend to stop smoking or never start. They tend to be more conscious about what they eat. Exercise helps you learn to relax. It can be a positive force that helps you to "do" other healthy behaviors without the feeling your life is being controlled by "don'ts". Regular exercise should be an integral part of your weekly lifestyle. It offsets the ill effects of sedentary living in our modern technological society and ensures that you are living at your physical potential. The benefits of exercise (see Table 1.1) are too numerous to discuss in depth here. However, the benefits will be elaborated on in subsequent chapters.

Life seems to be full of "don'ts" when it comes to health. Take a more optimistic perspective and make an active lifestyle and exercise "positive do's" in your life.

Table 1.1. Benefits of Exercise

- Strengthens the heart
- Decreases risk for cardiovascular diseases
- Decreases risk for some cancers
- Decreases risk for diabetes
- Helps to lower and/or maintain body fat
- Improves muscular strength and endurance
- Improves and maintains bone density
- Improves and maintains joint flexibility
- Reduces stress and muscular tension
- Improves quality of life
- Improves quantity of life

Later on in this book we will lay out the guidelines for developing a personalized fitness program. Designing a program is easy. However, exercising on a regular basis is not so easy. If exercise is fun, you will do it. So what is fun? It's working out with friends. It's setting goals and striving to meet them. It's successfully reaching these goals. It's the good feeling you get from using your body effectively. It is not necessarily smiling and laughing all the time. Often people say they never see people who are exercising smiling. However, if you look around at a movie or concert you'll probably notice that many members of the audience aren't smiling either. Does this mean they aren't enjoying themselves? The point is that fun comes in many different forms. The feeling of accomplishment, the ability to do more things with a sense of energy, all make for a fun life. Living life to the fullest is the payoff for your investment of effort and time in an active lifestyle involving regular exercise.

Exercise does not have to be grueling. Adopt strategies that make it fun and enjoyable and it will become a way of life.

IS EXERCISE FOR YOU?

What are your previous experiences with exercise and sports? Perhaps you have a negative attitude toward exercise. Through no fault of your own, past physical education or athletic experiences may have created this outlook. Experiences such as being punished with exercise, being chosen last as a team member, or being ridiculed or embarrassed because of poor sports skills may have kept you from getting involved in sports and exercise. The use of calisthenics or running laps to punish a participant is absolutely ridiculous. Allowing an inept performer to be heckled in a physical education class is inexcusable. No wonder so many people do not participate in sports or exercise. Who wants to do something that is associated with pain, punishment, or embarrassment? Obviously, not all people can excel in athletics or even make the team. Fortunately, though, physical educators and fitness instructors are now more attuned to gearing programs to your capabilities and limitations than in the past. Now there is more emphasis on lifetime activities that will deliver fitness benefits instead of focusing on competitive experiences. Regular fitness exercise for everyone is now widely recognized as an important component in physical education curriculums in colleges and universities.

Boys and men have always been encouraged to exercise and play sports, but for a long time physical exertion for girls was considered

The use of exercise for punishment leaves lasting negative impressions.

unladylike. Today, girls and women participate in competitive sports and all kinds of fitness activities. Research now clearly recognizes that women respond to vigorous physical training in the same way that men do. In fact, the research shows that the responses of men and women to vigorous activity are more similar than different.

The American College of Sport Medicine, the American Alliance for Health, Physical Education, Recreation and Dance, and the President's Council for Physical Fitness and Sports all emphasize the need for regular exercise as the basis for good health. Regardless of your past physical education experience or athletic background, this book is written for you. It provides all the basics to help you discover and improve your own physical capabilities. You don't have to be athletic to be physically fit.

A WAY OF LIFE

You don't have to be athletic to be physically fit.

Traditionally, organized athletics have tended to develop superfit competitors for the entertainment of a physically inept society. Programs that reward the best and disenchant the rest leave the majority ungratified, and even alienated. Such a philosophy, particularly in regard to exercise, has forced more people into the inept and physically unfit category. Why should you be relegated to be a mere spectator? You deserve the opportunity to develop the skills and abilities which can help you enjoy a full and active life. When you personally experience feeling better as a result of regular exercise and the sense of accomplishment of doing something good for yourself, you will become a convert.

WHAT IS PHYSICAL FITNESS?

Most authors define **physical fitness** as the capacity to carry out everyday activities (work and play) without excessive fatigue and with enough energy in reserve for emergen-

PHYSICAL FITNESS:
A physiologic state blending health-related and skill-related components which reflects the body's ability to meet physical challenges with vigor and resist diseases associated with sedentary living.

cies. Emphatically, this definition is inadequate given our modern way of life. By such a definition, almost anyone can be classified as physically fit. The typical banker, merchant, nurse, or student can probably hustle to catch a bus, work at their job all day, run up an occasional flight of stairs to be on time for a meeting, or play in a weekend softball game. Nevertheless, such a definition is not acceptable when we consider how inactive most Americans are in today's world. In other words, for most Americans being able to meet the light physical demands of their, mostly sedentary, daily lives is not an acceptable definition for physical fitness.

Physical fitness is more accurately defined as the capability of the heart, lungs, muscles, and other body systems to function at optimal levels such that the body is capable of enduring the demands of enthusiastic participation in daily tasks along with recreational activities and other unplanned physical demands or emergencies as they arise. Optimal physical fitness makes possible a lifestyle that the unfit cannot enjoy. Developing and maintaining physical fitness requires moderate to vigorous effort. As you will learn later on in this book, you do have to huff and puff a little. However this does not mean punishing, exhaustive exercise. It means working out well within your capabilities. You will learn that the benefits of being physically fit are well worth the exertion and sweat required.

A WAY OF LIFE

Optimal physical fitness makes possible a lifestyle that the unfit cannot enjoy.

WHAT ARE THE COMPONENTS OF PHYSICAL FITNESS?

Strength, muscular endurance, flexibility, cardiorespiratory endurance, and body composition are the basic health-related components of physical fitness (see Table 1.2). These five characteristics are required for the healthy functioning of the body. Another trait, motor skill performance, is often cited as a sixth fitness component. It refers to an individual's general athletic skills. While athletic skill is related to the other components of fitness, our main concern is with the health-related components. A rating of "good" in all of these areas indicates an acceptable level of physical fitness. Chapter 3 will assist you in determining your present fitness status. For now, we will briefly define each component to clarify its role in physical fitness.

Table 1.2. Components of Physical Fitness

- Muscular Strength
- Muscular Endurance
- Flexibility
- Cardiorespiratory Endurance
- Body Composition
- Athletic Skill / Motor Ability

Muscular Strength

Muscular strength is probably the most familiar component of fitness. It is the maximal amount of force that can be generated by a muscle or group of muscles and is typically assessed by determining how much weight a person can lift only one time. Resistance training or more specifically, strength training, is the mode of exercise used to increase muscle strength and in addition, can cause **muscle hypertrophy**.

Strength is fundamental in all sports. A lack of reasonable strength can obviously contribute to poor performance. Strength often seems to be lacking in the upper arms and shoulder region, especially in women. A lack of upper body strength can directly impair the

> **MUSCULAR STRENGTH:**
> The maximal amount of force generated by a muscle or group of muscles.

> **MUSCLE HYPERTROPHY:**
> An increase in the size of muscle that occurs in response to physical activity. Bodybuilders exhibit extreme muscle hypertrophy

ability to powerfully swing a golf club or tennis racket, not to mention make carrying out many daily activities more difficult. The lower body is typically stronger since it bears the weight of the rest of the body and is responsible for moving us around throughout the day.

Properly designed resistance training programs, such as working with barbells, are efficient means for gaining strength. In Chapter 7 we discuss resistance training techniques for the development of muscular strength.

Muscular Endurance

This trait is often used synonymously and incorrectly with strength. **Muscular endurance** is the capacity of a muscle to contract repeatedly over a period of time. Also, it refers to the ability of the muscle to hold a fixed, or static, contraction. In other words, it is the ability to apply strength and sustain it. Maintaining correct posture throughout the day regardless of whether you are sitting, standing or moving is one of the best examples of muscular endurance. Your ability to perform as many pull-ups as possible or to hold a bent arm hang is another indication of your muscular endurance. The capacity of your legs to perform in an endurance race, your arm to repeatedly swing a tennis racquet, or your hands to grip a

You will reach the point at which you will be working out not because you have to, but because you want to.

MUSCULAR ENDURANCE:
The capacity of a muscle to contract repeatedly or to hold a fixed or static contraction over a period of time.

golf club firmly and consistently throughout a round of golf are also examples of muscular endurance. Even activities around the home, such as shoveling snow, washing windows, painting, and cleaning house, all require some degree of prolonged muscular exertion. In Chapter 7 you will learn ways to improve muscular endurance.

Flexibility

Flexibility is the ability to move joints freely through a wide range of motion. In other words, it reflects a person's ability to bend, stretch, and twist. It is advantageous to possess good flexibility at all the various joints of the body. Maintenance of good joint mobility can decrease the risk for muscle injury and soreness. In contrast, inflexible joints and muscles increase the risk. For example, the need for flexibility varies with your specific needs. In swimming, shoulder and ankle flexibility is

important for efficient movement through the water. In karate the muscles of the legs, arms, and abdomen need a full range of movement. Even walking and jogging, seemingly effortless movements, require some degree of elasticity in the major muscle groups. Chapter 8 explains ways in which you can improve this component of physical fitness.

Cardiorespiratory Endurance

Although the physical fitness components discussed above are important, **cardiorespiratory endurance** is the most essential physical

Cross-country ski machines offer an excellent cardiorespiratory workout.

fitness component. Your life depends on the capacity of your cardiovascular system and lungs to deliver nutrients and oxygen to your tissues and to remove wastes. Efficient functioning of the heart and lungs is required for optimal enjoyment of activities such as running, swimming, cycling, and many of the vigorous sports. Most important, good cardiorespiratory endurance helps you to carry out everyday living with vigor. In Chapter 6 you will learn how to improve your cardiorespiratory endurance.

CARDIORESPIRATORY ENDURANCE:
The capacity of your heart, blood vessels, and lungs to function efficiently during vigorous, sustained activity such as running, swimming, or cycling.

Body Composition

Body composition refers to the make-up of the body in regard to fat and lean body tissues (such as muscle, connective tissues, and

Body composition is a key component of physical fitness.

bone). Depending on the methods used, various equations have been developed for estimating one's **relative body fat**.

BODY COMPOSITION:
The relative amounts of fat and lean body tissue (such as muscle, connective tissue, and bone) that make up your body. It is usually expressed as "Percent Body Fat".

RELATIVE BODY FAT:
The percentage of your total body weight that is fat weight. Body composition is usually expressed in terms of relative body fat (i.e. 18% body fat)

Relative body fat is the percentage of your total body weight that is fat. Carrying extra body fat not only affects physical prowess, it is also associated with poor health and physical fitness. Research evidence strongly suggests that physical inactivity is a principal cause for putting on excess weight, especially in the form of fat. Obesity increases one's risk for serious medical problems. Regular exercise is a positive approach to weight control. In fact, fit people burn more fat calories than the unfit both at rest and during exercise. This is due in part to their enhanced ability to utilize fats for energy during exercise as well as to a favorable body composition. In other words, fit individuals possess a higher percentage of muscle, which is 'hungry' tissue requiring more energy to sustain than fat tissue. Basically, the fit person at rest utilizes more calories than a less fit person thus decreasing the risk for fat gain. How fat are you? What is your desired weight? Methods for arriving at answers to these questions are presented in Chapter 3. Also, in Chapter 9 you will find updated information on the role of exercise and nutrition in maintaining your proper body weight.

Golf does not rank high as a fitness sport.

Athletic Skill Performance

Although a desirable attribute, having a high degree of **athletic skill** (motor ability) is not essential for maintaining a good level of physical health. Your ability to change direction rapidly, to control your balance, to react, and for your muscles to function in a coordi-

> **ATHLETIC SKILL/MOTOR ABILITY:** The ability of muscles to function harmoniously and efficiently, resulting in smooth coordinated muscular movement. A reflection of general athletic skill.

nated and efficient manner are all reflections of your general athletic skill. The ability of the nerves to receive and provide impulses that result in smooth coordinated muscular movements is a wonder of the human body. It is evident in the flawless performances of all elite athletes. Athletic skill can usually be evaluated with simple tests. Such tests as the vertical jump (requiring explosive power), an agility

run (requiring speed, balance, and agility), and 20 yard dash (requiring speed of body movement) have traditionally been used as tests of motor skill and general athletic ability. Since the main focus of this book is on the health-related components of physical fitness, further discussion of testing and development of athletic skills will not be included. However, for those interested in learning more about developing athletic skill visit Amazon's website and perform a book or video search using the name of the sport you are interested in or words such as "athletic development", "sport performance", "speed training", and "plyometric training".

WHY WORRY ABOUT PHYSICAL FITNESS?

Although the most opportune time for developing lifelong fitness habits is in the childhood years, it is in the late teens and early twenties that men and women start to develop a fitness consciousness. At this stage in life you have reached physical maturity; your body is at its natural peak of physiological functioning and health. However, a sedentary lifestyle can quickly begin to take its toll on the body. Just look around you, observe your friends, watch what happens as they enter their late twenties and early thirties. In many of them this natural fitness has begun to disappear. Lack of exercise is beginning to show its effect. An increase of body fatness, a loss of muscle tone, and a diminished energy level are some of the obvious signs of physiological deterioration. Unfortunately, our bodies are not programmed to handle the stresses of being sedentary or inactive.

Our modern lifestyle fosters unfitness. Many technological advances are intended to eliminate physical exertion from everyday activities. The automobile and television are key contributors to our sedentary lifestyle. We have also become accustomed to other automated energy savers: elevators, riding lawn mowers, motorized golf carts, snow blowers, and various remote control devices. The eighties brought us the home computer. Such technological advances enable us to carry out our everyday chores more easily. Microcomputers

When I was your age, I had to walk to the TV to change channels

Our modern lifestyle fosters unfitness.

not only enable us to keep our home or business records in order but also provide hours of enjoyable play with computer games of many kinds. Unfortunately, the rapid, repetitive movements required to manipulate the game controller does little for physical fitness. Working out regularly to maintain a healthy level of fitness enables us to enjoy these modern conveniences without suffering the physical deterioration associated with using them.

We live in a competitive society characterized by pressing domestic and international problems, business obligations, and deadline tensions. Smoking, alcohol, and drug abuse are all ways of escaping these pressures. Unfortunately, all of these escapes along with other poor habits/behaviors (see Table 1.3) have a negative impact on the physiological systems of the body and affect our state of health. Thus, there is a dire need, more than at any time in the history of humankind, to seek out stimulating exercise.

Table 1.3. Detriments to Good Health

- Inactivity
- Improper Nutrition
- Smoking
- Poor management of stress
- Excessive use of alcohol
- Drug abuse

Many men and women feel that their daily work provides them with enough exercise for fitness. Moving about the office, sitting at a computer for 8 to 10 hours or standing all day certainly seem to be physically taxing because we are often exhausted at the end of the day. While these tasks are forms of physical activity, they do not challenge the cardiorespiratory system adequately enough to keep the heart healthy and fit. If normal, day-to-day activities leave you fatigued at the end of the day, then you need the increased energy and vitality that comes from regular physical exertion.

Now that inactivity has been recognized as a threat to physiological well-being, some authorities have suggested that exercise may be the cheapest preventive medicine in the world. Researchers in medicine, nutrition, psychology, physiology, and physical education agree that exercise, properly performed, is necessary for maintaining functional physical fitness. No responsible health educator would ever suggest that exercise is a panacea. But it is clear that, just as we need food, rest, and sleep, we need daily regular exercise for the maintenance of our physical capacities. Physical fitness is not an end in itself but a means to an end. It provides the basis for optimal physiological health and gives us the capacity to enjoy a full life.

A WAY OF LIFE

Physical fitness is not an end in itself but a means to an end. It provides the basis for optimal physiological health and gives us the capacity to enjoy a full life.

WHAT DO YOU MEAN "ENJOY A FULL LIFE"?

People who keep fit greatly enlarge their fullness of living. They can do a day's work with ease; they can meet most emergencies; and they can extend their recreational activities to a second set of tennis, an extra nine holes of golf, or an extra mile of hiking on a trail.

Today, more and more people are becoming interested in individual activities and sports versus those requiring a partner or a team. Recreation such as backpacking, rollerblading, cross-country skiing, scuba diving, and mountain biking are popular. However, for complete enjoyment, participation in these activities requires a level of physical fitness beyond that needed in everyday life. To be pleasurable, a hike up a mountain or a scuba dive in a lake requires adequate physical conditioning. In other words, to enjoy your recreational endeavors fully, you need to be in shape.

A WAY OF LIFE

Being physically fit provides the robust health and the extra energy needed to fully appreciate the joys of life.

Being physically fit provides the robust health and the extra energy needed to fully appreciate the joys of life. Simply put, it adds a dimension of quality to our lives. We don't necessarily exercise just to prevent heart disease, to live longer, or to shed excess fat. Rather, we exercise to gain an increased physical capacity that allows us to enjoy a full life. Being able to do more things with competency and pleasure makes for a healthy and enjoyable existence.

SUMMARY

Your body needs regular physical activity to stay healthy. Unfortunately, our modern lifestyle does not require nor encourage moderate to heavy physical activity on a daily basis. Physical work and labor have been minimized in carrying out daily living. The use of all kinds of remote, automated, and innovative technical devices has diminished the use of the body physically.

Since ancient times, we have known that the body needs the regular nourishment of exercise. Active people tend to be healthy. Although not a guarantee of health, exercise if regularly practiced is looked upon more and more as the key to sound health and wellness. Exercise can be the "positive do" in your life. Do exercise!

Throughout this book, you will be given the knowledge to help improve the various components of physical fitness. Regular physical activity will certainly improve your health and help you achieve wellness and all its benefits. Life is a menu of choices. To paraphrase Per Olaf Astrand, an internationally famous exercise physiologist, if you chose not to exercise you should schedule a checkup with your physician to make sure your body can withstand the deterioration associated with a sedentary lifestyle. Hopefully after reading this book, you will be convinced that exercise is important to health and wellness. However, you must do more than just think about being active. You must act on your decision to adopt an active lifestyle and start to exercise. No one can do it for you and there is no magic pill you can take to make you physically fit. Good luck in your quest to make physical fitness a way of life.

2 Exercise Myths and Misconceptions

A frustrating (yet often amusing) dimension of physical fitness and exercise is the way supposed 'facts' twist reality or exaggerate outcomes to fit our hopes and expectations. In other words, what exercise can actually accomplish has become intertwined with various myths and misconceptions over time. One role of the fitness professional is to get the correct information out to the public. Unfortunately, it is an uphill battle. To the fitness professional it is clear from magazine cover headlines and wacky infomercials on TV that large numbers of well-intentioned people are not being given the straight story.

A WAY OF LIFE

Where do you typically get your fitness information? Infomercials and grocery store check-out line magazines may steer you in the wrong direction. Always check the credibility of your sources.

In this chapter we will attempt to clear the air by offering some of the more common myths and misconceptions that just won't die. Read through the following questions and see how your answers compare to those in the corresponding sections of this chapter.

- Will exercising one area of the body "spot reduce" the fat from that area?
- If I train to improve my muscle strength will my muscles get big and bulky?
- Will certain pieces of equipment or exercise techniques build longer, leaner muscles?

- Is low intensity exercise like walking better for burning off fat than higher intensity exercise like jogging?
- Do you have to exercise for at least 40 minutes in order to start burning off body fat?
- What is the best time of day to exercise?
- Does exercise allow for an "eat as you like" attitude?
- Does muscle turn into fat when you stop exercising?
- Will stretching prevent muscle soreness?
- Will a good runner also be a good all around athlete?
- In order to run a given distance faster, do you need to train by running longer distances?
- Do you need to be adept in a sport before you begin an exercise program to improve in the sport?
- Should you get in shape before you start lifting weights?
- Can everyone who exercises get "ripped" (i.e. super lean)?
- Is it true that men and women should train differently?
- Does buildup of lactic acid cause the muscle soreness you experience hours after exercise?

IS IT POSSIBLE TO SPOT REDUCE FAT?

Wouldn't it be great if we could choose a part of our body that carries more than optimal body fat and perform an exercise to get rid of the fat from that specific area? Yep, it would be great, but, nope, it won't happen. Genetics and gender tend to dictate where our bodies prefer to store fat. The best plan for reducing body fat boils down to expending more calories than you take in. This involves performing moderately intense aerobic exercise coupled with focused attention to what goes into your mouth. Resulting fat losses occur in a general pattern throughout the body, not simply in the regions surrounding the muscles used in your exercise program.

If you perform abdominal curls for 1 hour you will not specifically reduce the fat from around your belly. On the other hand, one hour of cardiorespiratory exercise like running is a great way to burn calories. Any fat lost would be in a general pattern, not targeted at the site of your working muscles.

Subcutaneous fat lies directly underneath the skin and is present in varying thicknesses. While cardiorespiratory endurance exercise steadily expends calories and helps reduce this layer, strong, toned muscles found underneath can be developed at the same time through

SUBCUTANEOUS FAT:
The layer of fat that lies directly underneath the skin and is present in varying thicknesses.

resistance training. In fact, resistance training can help 'tone' the body by increasing the muscle mass underlying the subcutaneous fat. As body fat is lost the underlying muscles make the body feel firmer. Perhaps the legend of spot reducing arose as a result of combining aerobic exercise (and sound nutrition) with resistance training which made it seem as if fat was being selectively diminished in some areas of the body.

Combining cardiorespiratory exercise plus resistance training is an excellent way to 'tone' your body. 'Cardio' burns optimal amounts of calories to help reduce body fat while lifting weights changes the size and strength of your muscles.

WILL I GET BIG BULKY MUSCLES IF I LIFT WEIGHTS?

Lifting weights, which is one type of **resistance training**, can produce a myriad of

RESISTANCE TRAINING:
A type of training designed to make muscles stronger by forcing them to work against loads not normally encountered during daily activities. Resistance training exercises use barbells, dumbbells, weight plates, body weight, elastic bands, or anything else that makes performing movement more difficult.

results depending on the intensity, duration, and frequency of training. While muscles can certainly become larger as a result of lifting weights, building huge muscles similar to those seen in bodybuilders takes years of intense training and is not the typical result. Unfortunately, the fear of building big muscles is one misconception that prevents some women from lifting weights. While women can experience some subtle changes in muscle size with resistance training, they will experience much less muscle growth than their male counterparts. This is due primarily to the effects of the male hormone testosterone. Furthermore, the weight training programs that most individuals, both male and female, engage in are designed to improve muscle strength and are not bodybuilding programs. In other words, the main goal is to improve the ability of the existing muscle to produce more force not build massive muscles.

The weight training programs that most individuals, both male and female, engage in are designed to improve muscle strength and are not bodybuilding programs.

If by chance a particular weight training program is causing more muscle development than desired, it can be adjusted. For example, decreasing the amount of weight being lifted and/or the number of exercises performed will decrease the stimulus for muscle growth. It is important to remember that you have control over the results of your weight lifting program. Once you achieve the results you want from your weight lifting program, you simply maintain your level of muscle development.

DO SOME MACHINES OR EXERCISE TECHNIQUES BUILD LONGER, LEANER MUSCLES?

This myth seems to stem from a misunderstanding of a) genetics, b) anatomy, and c) muscular strength versus muscular endurance. Claims that a certain piece of exercise equipment or technique used in an exercise class can give you long, lean muscles are not true. Instead, your genes gave you the predisposition for 'long' (or 'medium' or 'short') bones and the associated muscles that attach to those bones. These bogus claims fail to explain what exactly happens to those 'long, lean muscles' that have now outgrown the bone/s. Unless the equipment/technique also elongated your bones (an impossible feat), your newfound muscles would be too long for your unchanged bones and simply sag!

Perhaps some confusion exists concerning muscular strength and how it differs from muscular endurance. Muscular strength training produces actual anatomical changes in the muscle fibers that will cause different degrees of **hypertrophy**. This is necessary to improve the muscle's ability to generate force and overcome resistance. Muscular endurance training, on the other hand, is concerned with improv-

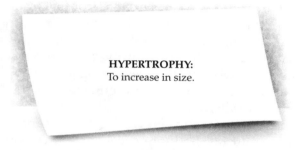

HYPERTROPHY:
To increase in size.

ing the muscle's ability to process oxygen and get rid of metabolic waste products during prolonged movement. Hypertrophy is generally not an outcome of highly repetitive mo-

Just because a person who performs a certain fitness activity has a specific 'look' that you want it does not necessarily mean that you will take on that same body if you engage in that activity. There are too many factors, such as genetics and nutritional practices, that cause us all to look the way we do.

tions. Perhaps that is how manufacturers/fitness promoters are defining long and lean? We think they are simply trying to sell their product. Just because a participant or instructor fits that definition of long and lean does not mean it was a direct result of a piece of equipment or a special class.

IS EXERCISING AT A LOWER INTENSITY BETTER FOR BURNING OFF BODY FAT?

Exercise equipment that allows you to choose from a variety of programs typically include a program called a "fat burner' or a 'fat burning zone'. This fat burning zone is performed at a lower intensity and for a longer duration than other programs. Ostensibly if you exercise in that zone you will be fueling your activity with a high proportion of fat and hence will lose fat weight more quickly. The theory behind this is not necessarily incorrect: it simply does not translate in practice. Here's why.

Our bodies have three choices of fuel from the foods we eat: protein, carbohydrate, and fat. In most instances, protein is not the primary fuel of choice (however, protein increases its role during very long duration, marathon-like exercise). Protein tends to be spared for other uses such as for building and repairing tissues of the body. That leaves carbohydrate and fat. Both are excellent sources of energy for exercise. When considering the unique contributions of carbohydrate and fat you can say that carbohydrates stored in muscle and circulating in the blood stream are a ready energy source. The body looks to carbohydrate almost exclusively to provide energy during sprint-type, all-out bursts of movement lasting very short periods of time. Fat, on the other hand, is more difficult to mobilize and increases its contribution during more moderate forms of exercise of longer duration. During low to moderately vigorous exercise both carbohydrate and fat contribute calories at various *percentages*. However, *percentage* of calories is not the same as *total* calories. This is where theory and practice diverge somewhat. Let's look at an example of the contribution of carbohydrate and fat calories during two exercise scenarios.

If a woman walked for 30 minutes, she would burn a total of 111 calories. At this intensity, fat contributes approximately 53 percent of the energy and carbohydrate contributes approximately 47 percent of the energy. You can see how, at the lesser intensities, the relative contribution of energy from fat is higher than that from carbohydrate. In this instance, 59 calories came from the breakdown of fat (53 percent of 111 calories). Sounds good, huh? Now, if the woman increased her exercise intensity by running for 30 minutes, the *percentage* contribution from fat decreases to 35 percent while that from carbohydrate increases to 65 percent. For someone trying to lose body fat it would seem that walking would be the better choice. However, running expends more calories *per minute* than does walking and therefore more *total* calories for the workout. The woman's total caloric expenditure running for 30 minutes is 276 calories. When comparing activities designed for weight loss it is the number of calories burned per minute that is important when the duration is kept the same. Walking for 30 minutes cost the woman 111

calories while running for the same amount of time cost 276 calories. Not only should this make running the evident choice of activity, but even when you look at the *percentage* of total calories burned from fat while running, that total is higher as well: 97 fat calories. Sounds even better, right?

Walking 30 minutes
53 percent fat 47 percent carbohydrate
Total kcalories = 111
53 percent of 111 calories = 59 calories from fat
Running 30 minutes
35 percent fat 65 percent carbohydrate
Total kcalories = 276
35 percent of 276 calories = 97 calories from fat

'Fat Burning', then, refers to a *percentage* contribution of fat and does not address *total* calories burned. The conclusion to draw from the previous example is that when you are capable of exercising at a higher intensity, you will always burn more calories per minute. In terms of losing body fat, this is the most efficient way to accomplish your goals.

As always, advance to the higher intensity activity gradually to avoid overuse injuries and to allow your body's systems to adjust properly. One benefit of exercising at a higher intensity is that you will be able to accomplish more in the same amount of time. Using the walking versus running example, if you walk at 4 miles per hour, you will complete 2 miles in 30 minutes. If you run at a pace of 6 miles per hour, you will complete 3 miles in that same 30 minutes.

DO I HAVE TO EXERCISE FOR AT LEAST 40 MINUTES BEFORE I BURN FAT?

Another myth concerning the role of exercise in losing body fat focuses on how long you should be active. Duration of exercise is one of the training specifics that can be manipulated in order to optimize body fat loss. Keep in mind, however, that whatever manipulations you make, it is the total number of calories expended per workout that truly leads to changes in body composition.

The truth of the matter is that, with the exception of sprint-type, brief bursts of energy (which are fueled by carbohydrate), both fats and carbohydrates are always being burned. This is true whether you are resting or exercising. Our bodies never rely solely on fats as a source of fuel, as carbohydrates must be present for fats to be broken down. The supply of carbohydrates stored in our muscles and circulating throughout our bodies is limited compared to our stored and circulating fats. As exercise duration increases our bodies rely more heavily on fats to contribute to our energy needs, thus sparing carbohydrates. A trained individual especially has the capability of utilizing fat stores sooner than an untrained individual. This prolongs the length of time the person can exercise before succumbing to exhaustion.

It is the total number of calories expended during exercise, not where those calories come from, that matters in fat loss. If your goal is to develop endurance and maintain movement for increasingly longer periods of time, it's good to know that fats will provide an increasing proportion of energy as your duration is extended. Endurance training facilitates this increased reliance on fats.

IS MORNING THE BEST TIME TO EXERCISE?

This misconception evolved as we developed an understanding of the fuels used during exercise. Since we are in a 'fasted state' upon waking, not having eaten for several hours, the thought was that without circulating carbohydrates in our bodies, we would rely more on fats as fuel. Once again, when you exercise you rely on both carbohydrates and fats for energy with the percentages of each varying depending on such factors as exercise duration and intensity. Remember, it is the total caloric expenditure of your exercise that counts when body fat loss is your goal, not where those calories come from.

A WAY OF LIFE

The best time to exercise is the time that is best for you.

Research as well as anecdotal evidence suggest that exercising in the morning does spell success for many. It is easier to maintain consistency in your training when you start your day with exercise, before life's distractions vie for your attention. Morning workouts also provide a time where you can plan your day and actually have a chance to think creatively without interruptions. But numerous people do not enjoy morning workouts, finding their energy levels are higher later in the day. They may prefer exercising mid-day as a break or early evening as a stress reducer following work. The bottom line is: the best time to exercise is the time that is best *for you*. Whenever your lifestyle and personality dictate you get the best workouts, whenever you are least likely to make excuses for missing a session…THAT is the right time for you.

CAN I EAT ANYTHING I WANT AS LONG AS I EXERCISE?

The energy in food is the 'calorie'…consuming excess calories causes increased body fat…exercise burns calories…THEREFORE, all I have to do to keep from gaining fat weight is to exercise, right??? Oh, don't we all wish this one were true. There are so many reasons to exercise, so many health benefits to be gained from vigorous movement. But the idea that exercise can justify anyone eating like there's no tomorrow just isn't one of them.

As is stated over and over in America, it is so easy to gain weight yet so difficult to lose it. This is a prime argument for preventing excess weight gain in the first place (beginning in childhood). However, for those who are learning this the hard way, a look at some numbers may clarify and motivate. In order to lose one pound of body fat, you must expend 3,500 calories more than you eat. Since the average

---

A WAY OF LIFE

In order to lose one pound of body fat, you must expend *3,500 calories* more than you eat.

---

runner burns approximately 100 calories per mile of running, that runner would have to cover 35 miles in order to lose one pound of fat through exercise alone. At an average of 6 to 7 miles per hour the runner would have to run between 5 and 6 hours in order to expend 3,500 calories. Got that kind of time? Not many of us do. This is why it is recommended that you eat mindfully and deliberately, being aware that what you put in your mouth in a very short period of time can take significantly longer to burn off. Wise eating choices plus regular vigorous exercise is the key to healthy levels of body fat.

A WAY OF LIFE

When a person loses one pound or more on a scale following a workout, very rarely is the loss one pound of fat. More likely the loss is due to water, which should be replaced by drinking fluids.

WILL MUSCLE TURN INTO FAT IF I STOP TRAINING?

Take a look at many former professional or collegiate athletes once they are finished competing. Their volume of daily exercise is greatly reduced while often their caloric intake stays higher than needed for their diminished energy requirements. Similarly, consider the general fitness enthusiast who becomes injured and fails to participate in an alternative activity during the healing process. The inevitable result of both these scenarios is a body that appears quite different from that of their more active days. A typical explanation for their newfound 'flab' is that their muscle has turned into fat. The truth is that this is not possible. Muscle is muscle, fat is fat and just as a steak will never be a hot fudge sundae, neither muscle or fat 'becomes' the other.

A WAY OF LIFE

Muscle is muscle and fat is fat; it's that simple.

Two physiological changes occur that make this transformation seem possible. First, when muscle tissue is not regularly overloaded by overcoming a resistance of some sort, it atrophies, or decreases in size and '**tone**'. Second, if the person eats more food than he or she

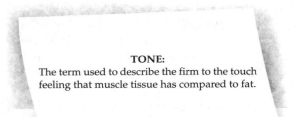

TONE:
The term used to describe the firm to the touch feeling that muscle tissue has compared to fat.

needs, the excess calories are stored as fat. Much of this fat is stored directly under the skin (subcutaneous fat), lying above the muscle and bone. This increased body fat adds to the appearance of 'softness'. However, this tissue that has decreased in size and tone is still muscle and the additional fat is still fat.

To avoid looking (and, frankly, feeling) like your muscle has turned into fat, it is important to remain highly active throughout life, maintaining as much lean tissue as possible and keeping body fat at healthy levels. This includes eating to fuel your current level of activity, not eating what you 'used to'.

WILL STRETCHING PREVENT INJURIES AND MUSCLE SORENESS?

A long-standing misconception that almost every physically active person has heard at least once in their lifetime is that they can remain at low risk for injury during sports and exercise if they engage in a stretching program. Additionally, when muscles are sore, people are frequently told to stretch in order to relieve their soreness or that stretching exercises will prevent soreness in the first place. Sounds like common sense and plausible, but there is no research to conclusively back up these assumptions.

The benefit derived from stretching that we can comfortably assert is its ability to temporarily increase mobility by making 'elastic' our muscles and their connective tissues which surround a joint. This then allows the joints where our bones meet one another to move in a full range of motion. Movement in general and exercise in particular are much more comfortable. Our bodies are capable of fuller motions and are not limited by inflexibility. Movements just feel good.

Flexibility is a fleeting state, however. Stretching your hamstrings today does not prepare them for action tomorrow. In order to maintain our joints' optimal range of motion, stretching needs to be performed regularly and correctly. Chapter 8 goes into detail on the appropriate training specifics for stretching for flexibility.

In the meantime, the recommendation for overcoming muscle soreness due to overtraining is 'active recovery'. This means continuing to move by performing lower intensities of your chosen activity versus resting your body until the soreness goes away. Actively recovering helps increase circulation, bringing nutri-

A WAY OF LIFE

It may sound counter-intuitive to stay active when you have muscle soreness, but that truly is an effective way to help your muscles feel better after overdoing it.

ents to the muscles and helping alleviate muscle spasms.

A WAY OF LIFE

Reducing the risk for injury involves having the highest levels of fitness in all components like muscular strength and endurance along with flexibility.

IF A PERSON IS A GOOD RUNNER, WON'T THEY ALSO BE GOOD AT EVERYTHING?

If you are highly accomplished in one aerobic activity there is no rule saying you should be highly accomplished in all aerobic activities. Sure, your cardiorespiratory endurance has been developed to a high degree, enabling your heart, lungs and blood vessels to deliver oxygen to your working muscles over extended periods of time. This conditioning does carry over from one aerobic activity to another. But in the process of training you have also taught your working muscles to repeat specific actions unique to that activity. These actions move the body in different angles and against varying forces that are distinct from all the other aerobic activities. Your central nervous system is involved in reinforcing those unique movements. The fitness tip in this scenario, then, is: *Training is specific.* A good runner spends the vast bulk of his training running,

A WAY OF LIFE

Training is specific.

using other aerobic activities when he needs a break either physically or psychologically. Cross training is an excellent strategy for preventing overuse injuries and for keeping your training fresh. Just don't think that spending hours on a bike will necessarily translate into making you a faster runner. For that you will have to hit the road on your feet, not your seat.

DO I HAVE TO TRAIN TO RUN FARTHER IN ORDER TO GET FASTER?

Once you feel comfortable with your cardiorespiratory endurance activity and have a good base of fitness you may want to increase your speed. Spending long periods of time piling up the miles will certainly improve your endurance. But performing more miles or yards at the same pace will only make you efficient *at that pace*. As stated above, training is specific and if you want speed you have to train for speed. Once or twice a week throw in some **speed work**. The easiest method involves simply picking up the pace during your nor-

> **SPEED WORK:**
> A method for increasing your speed during cardiorespiratory endurance activities that involves picking up the pace during your normal workout for a short period of time, backing off to your regular training zone when necessary, and repeated until you are able to train at the new, faster speed.

mal workout for a short period of time. When you feel like you are beginning to run out of breath, drop the pace back down to your regular training zone. Repeat this over and over during your speed workouts until you are able to perform the entire distance at your new faster pace.

Sprinting for short distances involves entirely different training methods. Interval training with intense work interspersed with periods of recovery are standard training techniques. However, these are more common in competitive sports scenarios than in training for general physical fitness.

DO I HAVE TO MASTER AN ACTIVITY BEFORE I USE IT IN TRAINING?

Some people avoid unfamiliar activities they think would be fun just because they are not 'good at them'. If we all had that approach, no one would be physically fit! The truth is, we all must start somewhere. Exercise programs addressing any of the five fitness components

are meant to progress gradually. In contrast with sports and athletics that require skill acquisition in order to feel competent, most fitness activities are easily mastered. For instance, because of their repetitive nature, virtually all aerobic activities are easily learned. Regular participation in your chosen activity not only conditions your body, you also gradually integrate any necessary skills simply by doing movements over and over. Your chosen activity eventually becomes second nature. When needed, fitness professionals can be consulted either in person or via the Web for smart tips that would give you more confidence when trying something new. (One benefit of being a novice at a fitness activity: the more inefficient you are, the more calories you burn!)

DO I NEED TO BE IN SHAPE BEFORE I START LIFTING WEIGHTS?

Along the same lines as the myth above, beginners should not delay starting a resistance training program until after they are 'in shape'. Being 'in shape' means you have developed acceptable levels of all five physical fitness components, one of which is muscular strength. You can't truly get in shape in the first place without engaging in strength training.

Perhaps you are concerned that you could hurt yourself by lifting too much weight. There is no reason to be fearful of the process if you are performing 'progressive resistance training'. This means that you incrementally increase the amount of weight a particular muscle group lifts only after your muscle/s adapt to the current weight.

It can be argued that muscular strength is the base on which all of the remaining fitness components are built. For example, muscles must be able to produce force in order to move the bones of the body. A minimum level of muscular strength is required for the nonstop movements involved in developing both muscular endurance and cardiorespiratory endurance. Additionally, strength training movements are usually performed in the largest safe range of motion possible in order to involve as much of the muscle group as possible. This contributes to the development of the fitness component of flexibility. Finally, developing muscular strength leads to increases in 'lean mass' which requires more calories than fat mass does. Coupled with the transformations that a more muscular physique make to improved body composition it is easy to see why strength training should be in on the ground floor of a program designed for all-around physical fitness.

> **A WAY OF LIFE**
>
> If we all performed heavy manual labor on a daily basis like our ancestors did, a formal program of strength training would not be necessary.

CAN EVERYONE GET SIX-PACK ABS?

Multiple factors contribute to the type of body you possess, with some of them stemming from your past and some from the present. Genetics help define your body type, from your bone structure to the ease with which you develop lean muscle mass. Additionally, we all have particular areas of our bodies where we tend to deposit fat easily and have a hard time losing it. All you can do about this is to say "'Thanks, Mom and Dad!" (you do get to choose the tone of voice you use, either sincere or sarcastic).

When it comes to acquiring a healthy level of body fat (yes, we all need certain levels of the stuff), let's say that nature loads the gun but we pull the trigger. By that we mean, even with a genetic propensity towards higher levels of body fat, we personally have the means of keeping those levels in the healthy range while developing optimal levels of lean muscle mass. The result is along the lines of 'Be All That You Can Be', choosing lifestyles that allow us to reach our optimally healthy levels of fat and muscle.

Muscle contributes to a lean appearance in a few ways. First, as muscle grows stronger, it hypertrophies or increases in size. This state

of hypertrophy is what we think of as muscle tone. The amount of subcutaneous fat lying on top of that muscle either creates the appearance of muscle definition or hides it. Genetics define your tendency to deposit subcutaneous fat at that site. Yet the amount of calories you expend with physical activity versus the amount of calories taken in when you eat will ultimately determine whether you have an extra layer of the stuff or not. Second, lean muscle mass is what is termed 'metabolically active': it is very 'hungry' tissue compared to fat tissue and requires more calories to exist. It stands to reason, then, that the more muscle mass you have the easier it will be to burn the calories you take in before they get the chance to become stored as fat.

> **A WAY OF LIFE**
>
> Muscle tissue is 'hungry' tissue, meaning it requires lots of calories both at rest and during work.

So what if you get to a healthy level of body fat through careful attention to the type and amount of food you eat in conjunction with a vigorous, active lifestyle and still don't consider yourself very lean? This may be the point at which you realize what you do and do not have control over. Learn to recognize when your body has reached its personal best and then strive to maintain those attributes for the rest of your life.

DO WOMEN AND MEN REQUIRE DIFFERENT TRAINING PROGRAMS?

When it comes to developing the five physical fitness components, both sexes should approach training the same way. The training principles apply equally to males and females. Now, there will certainly be differences between males and females in the amount of lean muscle mass they can acquire and their propensity for differing levels of body fat. There is also some evidence that females are better suited for endurance-type activities than are males. All of these, however, are differences in the *end result* of training, not in the *process* of training.

Certain pieces of exercise equipment may fit one sex better than the other, but usually adjustments can be made by adding or reducing padding or support platforms. With some equipment it may be as easy as simply inserting a rolled up towel where the body needs support or placing your feet in a different stance. Over the years there have been improvements in equipment design allowing each piece to accommodate different body sizes and types. This is accomplished through such modifications as seats that lift or lower, rods that slide in or out, range of motion limiters placed on moving parts, or elongating chains for accessories. Consequently there is no excuse for avoiding an exercise just because of your gender.

IS DELAYED ONSET MUSCLE SORENESS CAUSED BY A BUILDUP OF LACTIC ACID?

Delayed onset muscle soreness, or DOMS, resulting from overtraining or from launching into a new activity usually strikes 24 to 48 hours after your exercise bout. This soreness ranges from mildly irritating to almost debilitating, depending on the intensity or newness of your activity. DOMS is not caused by lactic acid, one of the byproducts of muscle contraction during strenuous or sprint-type activities. Lactic acid actually changes the pH levels in the blood, and as it builds up during strenuous exercise, pain receptors are triggered. Some exercisers describe this feeling as 'the burn'. Lactic acid is eliminated naturally from the site of the muscle. This elimination occurs rather quickly on its own but can be aided by continuing to move at lower intensity levels or even by gentle massage. The mechanical motion of the muscles contracting and relaxing helps pump and re-circulate the blood back to the heart and lungs.

The current theory about why DOMS occurs is that vigorous activity causes small tears in the muscle fibers. These small tears elicit an inflammatory response resulting in pressure on adjacent nerve endings. Until the inflammation dissipates these nerve endings send signals of discomfort to the brain. Make sure you understand the difference between this common muscle soreness and more serious muscle injury. Injury will produce immediate pain and should not be accompanied by continued movement. In the case of muscle injury, medical treatment should be sought.

SUMMARY

It's interesting how fitness myths and misconceptions get started. Frequently a myth begins as a fact that gets twisted and misinterpreted along the way. Talk to a dozen people who exercise and you may get a dozen suggestions on how to approach your fitness program. Unfortunately, listening to the wrong advice delays fitness gains or worse, leads to injuries. You would be wiser to apply the principles of training to your workout and remember the role genetics plays. Since exercise science is an evolving discipline and research is ongoing in all areas of fitness, look to reliable and factual sources for up-to-date information.

Getting Started

This chapter will assist you in evaluating your present level of physical fitness to identify your strengths and weaknesses. This evaluation will provide the basis for setting up an individualized exercise program that is safe, reasonable, and effective. Also, it will enable you to determine the effectiveness of your individualized exercise program.

The tests included in this chapter measure the health-related components of physical fitness. The tests are easy to administer and cover the major areas of fitness evaluation: body composition, flexibility, muscular strength, cardiorespiratory endurance, and muscular endurance. Although the physical fitness tests in this chapter have limitations, these tests will provide you with a rough estimate of your physical fitness status. Be sure to save your results so you can see how much you have improved as you progress in your exercise program.

Carefully read the following questions and after each one formulate the answer in your mind. If you don't know the answer, then read the chapter with the intent of finding the answer. If you did answer the question, then read to make sure your answer is correct and not a misconception you have about getting started on an exercise program.

- Why perform physical fitness testing?
- How often should you perform physical fitness testing?
- What tests would you use to assess the various components of physical fitness?
- How can you use the results from the various tests?

WHY PERFORM PHYSICAL FITNESS TESTS?

Physical fitness means more than bulging muscles or a trim waistline. A lean appearance, although desirable, does not necessarily reflect your physical fitness. No matter how you look, or even how strong you are, you have a low level of fitness if your heart is unable to meet the circulatory demands of prolonged work. Many men and women, for instance, appear very fit but tire easily while carrying out their everyday activities.

Each individual is unique, with different abilities in various physical and mental tasks. In addition, all people have their own physiological limitations. This chapter will help you develop a practical testing program for appraising your fitness so that you can set up a program that is appropriate for you.

A WAY OF LIFE

Don't be overly concerned with how you compare to others on the various physical fitness tests. We are all different and have our own unique set of physical capabilities.

It is only human to be curious about how you compare with others. Although physical fitness measurements afford you this opportunity, it is more important to use your data to help set up a reasonable program that meets your needs. Later on, you will want to repeat these tests to assess the effectiveness of your training program. Repeat testing can be fun and highly motivating. However it should not dominate a conditioning program. In other words, testing should not be done more than once every 6 to 8 weeks.

The classification charts presented in this chapter for the various tests can help you identify your strengths and weaknesses and provide you insight into your physical capabilities. In addition, it will help you evaluate the effectiveness of your training program, whether it involves running, swimming, weight training, or a combination of activities. Consequently, don't be overly concerned with what other people can or cannot do. The self-tests in this chapter will help you make your own before-and-after comparisons. Fitness is individual, so measure your own improvement and watch your own progress. By following the testing procedures carefully, you can find out whether you need to improve any or all of the components of physical fitness. Table 3.1 summarizes the reasons for periodic fitness testing.

Table 3.1. Reasons for Periodic Fitness Testing:

- To establish one's current fitness status
- Results can serve as a basis for setting realistic fitness goals
- Results can be used to design an individualized exercise program
- Results can be used to evaluate the effectiveness of a training program
- Results can provide motivation for starting and/or adhering to an exercise program

Finally, if you are in doubt about your state of health, check with your physician before attempting any of these vigorous tests. This is very important for persons over 30, especially for anyone who has not recently been physically active.

WHAT PHYSICAL FITNESS TESTS SHOULD I PERFORM?

The tests in this chapter have all been used successfully to measure the basic components of physical fitness. They were selected because they provide for uniformity in scoring, consistency in measuring, and overall ease in administering. Also, minimal time and equipment are required to perform these tests. In some cases you may have access to more extensive tests to evaluate your fitness. Regardless of what set of tests you use, going through a **test battery** can help you establish a fitness baseline.

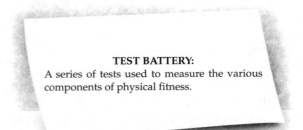

TEST BATTERY:
A series of tests used to measure the various components of physical fitness.

The tests are grouped into the following areas: (1) body composition, (2) flexibility, (3) muscular strength, (4) muscular endurance, and (5) cardiorespiratory endurance. The rationale for the tests and the instructions for carrying them out are presented in the sections that follow. It is important to keep track of the results of your testing for future comparison using a data sheet (see Figure 3.1). For your convenience we have included data sheets for you to fill out in Appendix E.

Following is a suggested order of testing. Make sure to follow the same order for the tests during both the initial testing and any follow-up testing. Also, note the length of rest periods you took between tests, and use the same rest periods when performing follow-up testing. Table 3.2 provides a list of the tests and the suggested order in which to perform them.

In each section you will find tables that list test results for men and women and provide scales on which you can rate your own performance. Remember not to get carried

Name: _____ Date: _____

Age: _____ Height: _____ Weight: _____

Chest Press (in pounds)

Measure 1 _____ Measure 2 _____ Measure 3 _____ Best of 3 _____

Best measure divided by body weight _____ (1 RM/body weight)

Norm category _____

Leg Press (in pounds)

Measure 1 _____ Measure 2 _____ Measure 3 _____ Best of 3 _____

Best measure divided by body weight _____ (1 RM/body weight)

Norm category _____

Body Composition (skinfold measures in millimeters)

	Measure 1	Measure 2	Measure 3	Average of 3 Measures
Triceps	_____	_____	_____	_____
Subscapula	_____	_____	_____	_____
Midaxillary	_____	_____	_____	_____
Suprailiac	_____	_____	_____	_____
Abdomen	_____	_____	_____	_____
Thigh	_____	_____	_____	_____
			Sum of 6 averages =	_____

Percent body fat (see Figure 3.3) _____

Norm category _____

Trunk Flexion (in inches)

Measure 1 _____ Measure 2 _____ Measure 3 _____ Best of 3 _____

Norm category _____

Push-ups (repetitions)

Number of push-ups in 1 minute _____ Norm category _____

Abdominal Crunches (repetitions)

Number of abdominal crunches in 1 minute _____ Norm category _____

1.5-Mile Run (in minutes:seconds)

Time for 1.5 mile run _____ Norm category _____

Step Test (heart rate)

Recovery heart rate 1:00 to 1:30 _____

Recovery heart rate 2:00 to 2:30 _____

Recovery heart rate 3:00 to 3:30 _____

Sum of 3 recovery heart rates (recovery index) _____

Norm category _____

Figure 3-1: Fitness Assessment Data Sheet

Table 3.2. Suggested Order of Testing

- Muscular Strength: Chest Press
- Muscular Strength: Leg Press
- Body Composition
- Flexibility: Trunk Flexion
- Muscular Endurance: Push-ups
- Muscular Endurance: Abdominal Crunches
- Cardiorespiratory Endurance: 1.5 Mile Run or Step Test

away comparing your scores to the scores in the tables or the performance of others. If you score low in all tests or only in one or two, consider the reasons, and design your training program to do something about it.

HOW CAN MUSCULAR STRENGTH BE DETERMINED?

Strength is traditionally measured by determining your **one-repetition maximum (1-RM)**, which is the amount of weight you can lift only one time. It is recommended that

ONE REPETITION MAXIMUM (1-RM): A commonly used measure of muscular strength. It represents a weight or resistance that is so heavy that a person can only successfully lift it one time.

beginners use resistance machines rather than free weights (barbells, dumbbells, etc.) to test strength. If free weights are going to be used, it is imperative that someone be present to help with testing. The two tests discussed here measure muscular strength of the upper and lower body.

A WAY OF LIFE

If free weights are going to be used during strength testing, it is imperative that someone be present to help.

Specifically the chest press measures muscular strength of the chest, shoulders, and arms, while the leg press measures the muscular strength of the hips and thighs. You can test the strength of other muscle groups if you would like. However, we highly recommend that you perform the chest and leg press tests before doing any others. Muscular strength is often taken for granted, as if it were something we are born with. However, building and maintaining muscular strength throughout life takes commitment and work.

Because strength can be greatly affected by one's size, the strength data in Table 3.3 are relative strength measures. In other words, to compare your numbers with those in the table you have to divide your 1RM weight by your body weight. For example, Sue's bench press is 100 pounds and she weighs 120 pounds. Sue's relative strength is 100 divided by 120, or 0.83. According to Table 3.3 her chest press strength is excellent.

Chest Press

Purpose: To determine the strength of the muscles of the chest, shoulders, and arms

Equipment: Chest press machine or, alternatively, a bench, bar, and weights

Test Setup: Prior to beginning the testing, perform a 3 to 5 minute warm-up of light activity involving movements of the legs and arms. After the warm-up, lie back on the bench and position hands about shoulder width apart on the handles/bar. Slide up or down on the bench so that your hands are positioned about nipple level and elbows are directly under the handles/bar. Your feet should be firmly planted on the floor slightly wider than shoulder width and your back should be flat on the bench. (see Figure 3.2)

Procedure: Place a light weight on the machine/bar and perform 8 to 10 practice

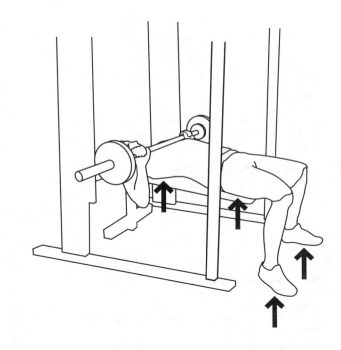

Figure 3.2b: Illustration of Proper Setup on Bench Press Test

lifts. After the practice lifts, place a weight that you feel you can lift once. As a rule of thumb, a good starting weight is 70% and 100% of body weight for women and men, respectively. Position yourself on the bench (see Test Setup) and attempt the lift. If the attempt was successful, add more weight. If unsuccessful, remove some weight. Take a 3-minute rest and perform another attempt. Continue this process until you have determined your 1-RM. (Note: The goal is to determine the 1RM in as few attempts as possible, so use your best judgment when increasing or decreasing the weights between attempts.) Refer to Table 3.3 for norms for chest press.

Improper Procedures: Holding your breath; not maintaining proper form while performing the lift; arching your lower back; lifting your buttocks off the bench; lifting one or both feet off the floor, twisting your torso on the bench

Leg Press

Purpose: To determine the strength of the muscles of the hips and thighs

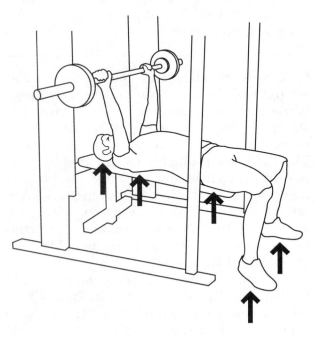

Figure 3.2a: Illustration of Proper Setup on Bench Press Test

Equipment: Leg press machine
Test Setup: It is assumed that you have already warmed up prior to performing the chest press. If not, then do so (see chest press: test setup). Adjust the machine so that at its lowest position, your knees make a 90-degree angle. (see Figure 3.3)

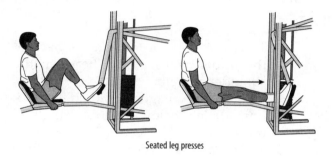

Seated leg presses

Figure 3.3: Proper Setup on Leg Press Test

Procedure: Place a light weight on the machine and perform 8 to 10 practice lifts. After the practice lifts, place a weight that you feel you can lift once on the machine. As a rule of thumb, a good starting weight is 130% and 200% of body weight for women and men, respectively. Position yourself on the leg press machine (see Test Setup) and attempt the lift. If the attempt was successful, add more weight; if unsuccessful, remove some weight. Take a 3-minute rest, and perform another attempt. Continue this process until you have determined your 1-RM. (Note: The goal is to determine the 1RM in as few attempts as possible so use your best judgment when increasing or decreasing the weights after attempts.) Refer to Table 3.3 for norms for the leg press.
Improper Procedures: Holding your breath; not maintaining proper form while performing the lift; lifting your buttocks off the seat or pad; not going deep enough (less than a 90-degree knee angle) during the press

Table 3.3 Norms for Muscular Strength Relative To Body Weight
(1 RM/body weight)

	Women		Men	
	Chest Press	Leg Press	Chest Press	Leg Press
Excellent	≥ 0.81	≥ 1.75	≥ 1.31	≥ 2.30
Good	0.75–0.80	1.45–1.74	1.11–1.30	2.10–2.29
Average	0.70–0.74	1.31–1.44	1.00–1.10	2.00–2.09
Fair	0.41–0.69	1.00–1.30	0.5–0.99	1.61–1.99
Poor	≤ 0.40	≤ 0.99	≤ 0.49	≤ 1.60

HOW CAN BODY COMPOSITION BE EVALUATED?

Weighing yourself on a scale tells you nothing about your body composition because it does not discriminate between **fat weight** and **lean body weight** (composed primarily of muscles and bones). Thus, trying to track changes in body fat based on body weight can

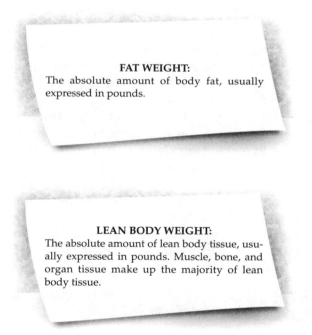

FAT WEIGHT:
The absolute amount of body fat, usually expressed in pounds.

LEAN BODY WEIGHT:
The absolute amount of lean body tissue, usually expressed in pounds. Muscle, bone, and organ tissue make up the majority of lean body tissue.

be misleading and frustrating. For example, certain types of exercise programs can increase lean body weight and decrease fat weight, resulting in little change in body weight even though fat was lost. The methods commonly

Weighing yourself on a scale tells you nothing about your body composition.

used to determine body composition involve underwater weighing or skinfold measurements. Underwater weighing, or its newer equivalent using a piece of equipment known as the Bod Pod, is considered the "gold standard" for determination of body composition. However, both require expensive equipment and a trained technician. Skinfold measures are determined using relatively inexpensive **skinfold calipers**, which measure the thickness of

SKINFOLD CALIPERS:
An instrument used in body composition assessment to measure the thickness of a fold of skin and its underlying subcutaneous fat.

fat lying immediately below the surface of the skin. Unfortunately, skinfold measurement is also best performed by experienced professionals. These services are commonly offered by university physical education departments, hospital wellness programs or health/fitness centers at a small cost (generally $10 to $50). If possible, we highly recommend that you get your body composition measured prior to beginning or changing your exercise program. For your information we have included instructions on the proper technique for measuring skinfolds and the location of six sites commonly measured.

It is highly recommended that you get your body composition measured prior to beginning or changing your exercise program.

The skinfold measures can be used in two ways. One is to estimate your percent body fat.

Another interesting way, one that can be less demoralizing for those who are self-conscious or don't want to know their body fat, is simply to use the sum of the skinfolds. Keeping track of changes in the sum of the skinfolds lets you know whether you are gaining or losing fat over time. Furthermore, it can give you an indication of where on the body you are losing the most fat.

The anatomical landmarks for the six skinfold sites are as follows (also see Figure 3.4):

1. *Triceps:* A vertical fold on the back of the upper arm midway between the shoulder and elbow joint
2. *Subscapula:* A diagonal fold on the back immediately below the lower angle of the scapula
3. *Midaxillary:* A vertical fold on the side of the body (mid-armpit) at the level of the lower end of the sternum
4. *Suprailiac:* A diagonal fold on the side of the body just above the top of the hip bone (crest of the ilium)
5. *Abdomen:* A vertical fold on the abdomen approximately two centimeters (one inch) to the side of your navel.
6. *Thigh:* A vertical fold on the front of the thigh midway between the hip and knee joints.

Procedure: Skinfold measures are taken on the right side of your body (even for left-handed persons) while you are standing. At the appropriate site (see Figures 3.4) grasp a fold of skin using the thumb and forefinger of your left hand. Most of the skinfolds taken at the different sites are vertical folds, while the folds taken at the subscapular and suprailiac sites are diagonal. The diagonal folds are picked up on a slight slant that follows the natural folding of the skin. While holding the skinfold with the left thumb and index finger, place the caliper pinchers over the fold about a 1/2 inch below your fingers. (NOTE: It is important to remember to maintain holding the fold with your left hand throughout the measuring process.)

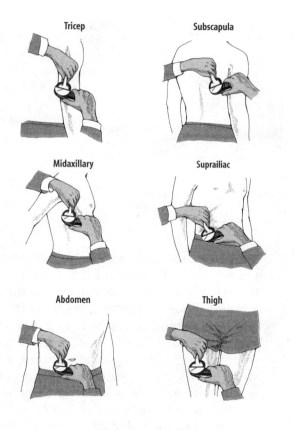

Figure 3.4: Skinfold Sites

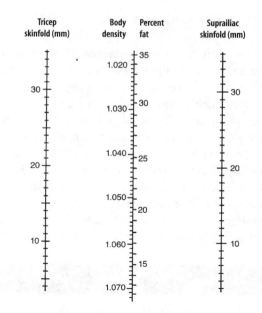

Source: Based on data from (1) A. W. Sloan et al., *Journal of Applied Physiology* 17 (1962): 967, and (2) J. F. Brozek et al., *Annals of the New York Academy of Science* 101 (1963): 113.

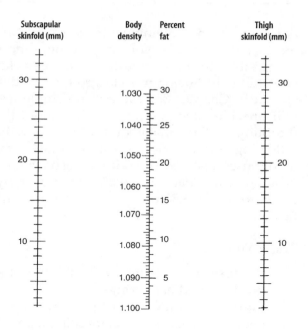

Figure 3.5 a, b: Nomograms for Percent Body Fat

Release the spring lever on the calipers and quickly (usually within 2 seconds) take the skinfold measurement. Move to the next skinfold site. Rotate from site to site until you have taken three measures for each. Average the three measures for each site and then add the averages together to get your sum of the skinfold measures. If you would like to estimate your percent body fat, use the specific skinfold measures noted on the nomograms, depending on your gender (see Figure 3.5 A or B). Table 3.4 gives the norms for body composition.

Improper Procedures: Taking skinfold measures on the left side of the body; not maintaining the fold with the left hand; placing the skinfold pinchers less than or more than a half inch from your fingers when taking the measure; taking longer than 2 seconds to read the caliper measurement.

Table 3.4 Norms for Body Composition (% body fat)

	Women	Men
Desirable	18%–29.9%	12%–19.9%
Overfat	30.0% to 34.9%	20.0% to 24.9%
Obese	≥ 35%	≥ 25%

HOW IS FLEXIBILITY MEASURED?

Flexibility assessment involves measuring the maximum range of motion at a joint. Flexibility can be affected by muscle, tendon, and ligament tightness, which can limit movement about the joint. The loss of the ability to bend, twist, and stretch is often a result of muscle disuse, such as in excessive periods of sitting or standing. Sedentary living habits can lead to loss of flexibility, lower back pain, and muscle imbalances. For example, shortening of the hamstrings (the muscles located in the back of the thighs) is very common. Extreme flexibility,

Figure 3.6: Trunk Flexion Test

A WAY OF LIFE

The loss of flexibility is often the result of muscle disuse.

---

however, has no advantage. If your joints are too loose or flexible, you may become more susceptible to joint injuries. Exercises for stretching the major muscle groups are discussed in Chapter 8. Although no single test will provide adequate information about the flexibility of all the major joints of the body, the following trunk flexion test is the most commonly used test and provides a reasonable indication of low back and hamstring flexibility. Refer to Table 3.5 for the norms for trunk flexion.

Trunk Flexion

Purpose: To measure the flexibility of the low back and hamstrings

Equipment: Ruler, 6- to 8-inch stairstep or bench, powder or chalk, masking tape

Setup: Place the ruler on the edge of the stairstep or bench so that the 6-inch mark is aligned with the edge (see Figure 3.6). Tape the ruler in place.

Procedure: Sit with your legs fully extended and the bottoms of your feet (shoes off) flat against the stairstep or bench, with the ruler between your feet (see Figure 3.6). Be careful not to knock the ruler loose. Put chalk or powder on your middle fingertips. Place hands over the ruler, one hand on top of the other, aligning your middle fingers. Slowly exhale and extend (stretch) your arms and hands forward as far as possible while maintaining the finger alignment and straight legs. Allow your head to curl forward and low back to round as you reach. Pause when you can reach no further and tap the ruler with your chalked middle fingertip. Do not bounce to gain extra distance. Return to the starting position and determine where your fingertip touched the ruler. Read the ruler at the farthest edge of the chalk mark. Repeat two or three times and record your best score.

Improper Procedures: Not maintaining middle finger alignment; not pausing in the full reach position (for example, bouncing to get extra distance); bending at the knees.

Table 3.5 Norms for Trunk Flexion (inches)

	Women	Men
Excellent	≥ 13.0	≥ 12.0
Good	11.0–12.9	10.0–11.9
Average	9.0–10.9	8.0–9.9
Fair	7.0–8.9	6.0–7.9
Poor	0.0–6.9	0.0–5.9

HOW CAN MUSCULAR ENDURANCE BE ASSESSED?

The two tests discussed here measure muscular endurance of key muscle groups of the body. The push-up test assesses the muscular endurance of the muscles of the chest, arms, and shoulders. The abdominal crunch test measures the muscular endurance of the abdominal muscles. The abdominal muscles play an important role in maintaining correct posture, thus reducing the risk for lower-back pain. Additionally, the abdominal muscles have been labeled by some as the center of strength. Working in conjunction with the back extensor muscles, the abdominal muscles stabilize the torso to provide a rigid base around which the muscles of the extremities can apply force. These muscles play a vital role in many of the activities of daily living.

Remember the purpose of these tests is to help you assess your muscular endurance and, most important, to determine your own baseline for future comparison.

Push-ups

Purpose: To test the muscular endurance of the muscles of the chest, arms and shoulders.

Equipment: Timing device

Procedure: Kneel on all fours, with hands about shoulder width apart and positioned beneath your shoulders. Extend your legs back, with the weight on your toes and the body in a straight line (see Figure 3.7). As you bend at the elbows, lower your body as a unit until you achieve a 90-degree bend at the elbows. Keeping your back straight, press yourself to the up position. Repeat this procedure as many times as you can for 1 minute. (NOTE: If you are unable to perform one standard pushup, your muscular endurance is poor. In order to establish a baseline measure with this test, use a modified pushup. Kneel on all fours, with hands about shoulder width apart and positioned beneath your shoulders. Extend your legs back, but this time, place

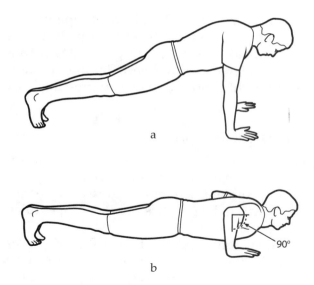

Figures 3.7a and b: Push-up Start and End Positions

your weight on your bent knees, with your body in a straight line (see Figure 3.8). As you bend at the elbows, lower your body as a unit until you achieve a 90-degree bend at the elbows. Keeping your back straight, press yourself to the up position. Refer to Table 3.6 for norms for push-ups.

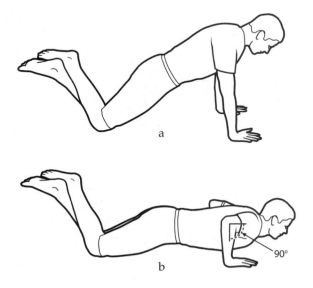

Figures 3.8a and b: Modified Push-up Start and End Positions

Improper Procedures: Not keeping your body straight; allowing your body to sag or peak upwards; not going down to a 90-degree elbow bend; failing to fully straighten your arms when pressing back up.

Abdominal Crunches

Purpose: To determine the muscular endurance of the abdominal muscles

Equipment: Exercise mat, two cardboard pieces (3 by 6 inches) masking tape, ruler, timing device

Test Setup: Align the cardboard pieces with the mat's edge about hip width apart as shown in Figure 3.9 and secure them to the mat with masking tape (see Figure 3.9).

Procedure: Lie on your back with arms straight and resting on the floor by your side. The palms of your hands should be turned down toward the floor. Position your body so that your fingertips just touch the leading edge of the cardboard pieces. Draw your feet back toward the buttocks until they are flat on the floor (knees bent). The angle of your legs to your thighs should be approximately 90 degrees (see Figure 3.9a). Just prior to

beginning the test round your lower back so that it touches the mat, maintaining contact throughout the test. Tuck your chin to your chest. Contract the abdominal muscles, lifting your shoulder blades while sliding your hands along the cardboard pieces until your fingertips touch the edge of the mat. (See figure 3.9b) Your hands must remain in contact with the cardboard throughout the crunching movement. Return to starting position and repeat this procedure as many times as possible within 1 minute. Resting is permitted, but only in the starting position. Refer to Table 3.6 for norms for abdominal crunches.

Improper Procedures: Not crunching enough to reach the end of the mat; not returning to the starting position between repetitions; not keeping your hands on the cardboard; holding your breath during the test

HOW CAN CARDIORESPIRATORY ENDURANCE BE TESTED?

As discussed in Chapter 1, cardiorespiratory endurance depends on the ability of the heart to pump blood, the lungs to oxygenate the blood, and the muscles to utilize the oxygen delivered by the blood. Therefore, sustained muscular activity is possible only through the effective functioning of three major systems: the cardiovascular, the respiratory, and the muscular systems. Various tests involving vigorous physical movement that

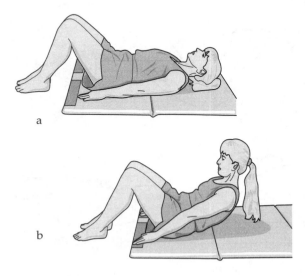

Figure 3.9a and b: Abdominal Crunch Test

Table 3.6 Norms for Muscular Endurance (repetitions)

| | Men | | Women | |
	Crunches	Push-ups	Crunches	Push-ups*
Excellent	≥ 54+	≥ 40	≥ 45	≥ 24
Good	46–53	34–39	39–44	16–23
Average	41–45	28–33	31–38	10–15
Fair	36–40	22–27	26–30	4–9
Poor	0–35	0–21	0–25	0–3

* Norms for standard pushup.

make increased demands on the heart and lungs have been devised to assess cardiorespiratory endurance.

Procedures for determining aerobic capacity (i.e. cardiorespiratory endurance) in the laboratory are complex, time-consuming, and impractical for testing large numbers of people. Exercise physiologists, therefore, have attempted to develop **field tests** that can be substituted for laboratory tests. Field tests like the 1.5-mile run and step test have correlated well

FIELD TESTS:
Tests that take place outside the laboratory.

with laboratory-determined values for cardiorespiratory endurance. Thus field tests make it quite easy to determine your cardiorespiratory endurance and to detect changes due to training. The procedures for performing the 1.5-mile run and the step test are described below. If you are in fairly good shape and are comfortable jogging or running, then perform the 1.5-mile run. However, if you are sedentary and/or not comfortable running, then perform the step test. Both will give you a good indication of your cardiorespiratory endurance.

1.5 Mile Run

Most field tests of cardiorespiratory endurance utilize running or walking. Bruno Balke, a physician-physiologist, has demonstrated that an adequate estimate of aerobic ca-

pacity is possible after as little as 10 minutes of running at a near maximal effort. If the runs are completed in less than 8 to 10 minutes, a significant amount of energy comes from anaerobic sources. But if maximum work is performed for 10 to 20 minutes, the energy comes predominantly from the utilization of oxygen. Therefore, distance runs of 1.5 miles, which typically take 10 to 20 minutes to complete, are valid cardiorespiratory endurance field tests, especially for those who have some experience in running.

Purpose: To test the capability of the respiratory and cardiovascular systems to meet the energy demands of your body during aerobic activity.
Equipment: Timing device
Setup: Measure a 1.5 mile course or locate a high school/university track
Procedures: After a 3- to 5-minute warmup (see Chapter 5), measure the time it takes to run the 1.5 miles. Pacing is very important. You do not want to start out running and finish walking, nor do you want to start too slow and finish with energy left over. Try to maintain a consistent running pace that allows you to complete the course in a minimum amount of time. Refer to Table 3.7 for norms for the 1.5-mile run. If you are not accustomed to running or do not feel you can run the entire 1.5 miles, then use the step test (see the following) to assess your cardiorespiratory endurance.
Improper Procedures: Not finishing the 1.5 mile course.

Step Test

Another useful procedure for assessing your cardiorespiratory endurance is the step test, a heart-rate recovery measure. Stepping on and off a bench for a 3-to 5-minute time period at a selected cadence has long been used for rating a person's physical capacity for hard work and for evaluating the effects of training. Although not considered the best measure of cardiorespiratory endurance, the heart rate during recovery from a standardized step test is a simple way to evaluate the heart's response to exercise. The faster your heart rate recovers after the standardized exercise bout, the higher your fitness rating. The test is easy to administer on an individual basis or to a large group. It takes little time, does not require special skills to perform, and requires a minimum of equipment.

Purpose: To indirectly assess cardiorespiratory endurance based on your heart rate recovery

Equipment: 16- to 18-inch bench (or sturdy chair, locker room bench, bleachers), timing device, metronome (Note: If a metronome is not available practice repeating "up up down down" in 2-second intervals.)

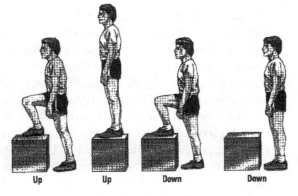

Figure 3.10: Step Test

Procedure: Start the metronome, which should be set at 120 beats per minute. Start the timing device with your first step beginning with the right foot up, then the left foot up; then the right foot down, and the left foot down (see Figure 3.10). This four-count sequence represents one complete step. At 120 beats per minute, you will execute 30 steps per minute. It is permissible to change the "up" foot during the test. Continue the test for 3 minutes, keeping tempo with the metronome. Be sure to straighten your knees as you step up onto the bench.

Upon completion of the 3 minutes of stepping, begin your recovery period by immediately sitting on a chair or straddling the bench and resting. One minute

into the recovery period, count your pulse for 30 seconds (e.g. 1:00 to 1:30), and record it. Repeat this procedure for the second (2:00 to 2:30) and third (3:00 to 3:30) minutes of recovery. To take your pulse, press lightly with your index and middle fingers on the inside of your wrist on the thumb side or just below your jawbone in the hollow beside the Adam's apple (see Figure 3.11)

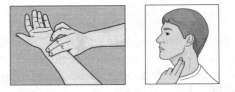

Figure 3.11: Wrist and Neck Pulse Sites

To determine your recovery index sum the three 30-second pulse measurements and compare your personal recovery index for the step test with the norms in the Table 3.7.

Improper Procedures: Not keeping the cadence of 30 step executions per minute; failing to straighten your knees to full extension on the up steps; not counting your pulse accurately.

HOW CAN I USE THE RESULTS FROM THESE FITNESS TESTS?

Once you have evaluated your fitness or skill level for each component, use the informa-

Table 3.7 Norms for Cardiorespiratory Endurance

	Women		Men	
	1.5-mile run (min.)	Step-test (bpm)	1.5-mile run (min.)	Step-test (bpm)
Excellent	≤ 13:00	≤ 135	≤ 10:45	≤ 132
Good	13:01–14:19	136–153	10:46–11:30	133–147
Average	14:20–15:38	154–170	11:31–12:15	148–162
Fair	15:39–16:57	171–187	12:16–13:00	163–177
Poor	≥ 16:58	≥ 188	≥ 13:01	≥ 178

tion as a starting point for developing your personal fitness program. It is not unusual to find that you possess strengths in some areas and weaknesses in others. Very few individuals rate as excellent for every fitness component, yet all of us should strive to reach our highest potential in each them. For example, if you rate "excellent" for cardiorespiratory endurance but your muscular strength and muscular endurance ratings were "poor", then your training program should focus on improving your strength and endurance and at a minimum maintaining your cardiorespiratory status.

A WAY OF LIFE

Very few individuals rate as excellent in all areas of physical fitness. However we should strive to reach our highest potential in them all.

After you have participated regularly in any program for approximately six weeks, you may wish to perform these self-assessments once again to measure any improvements made. Of course, you should feel and see improvements after undertaking a fitness program. However, actually measuring and charting the changes can help to further motivate you. In the example shown in Figure 3.12, on May 15, muscle strength in the chest press increased 25 pounds and percent body fat had decreased 10 percent when compared to the initial baseline measures that were taken on January 1. We have included a "Personal Physical Fitness Progress Chart" and directions on how to use it in Appendix A so that you can plot your results each time you reassess your fitness level.

On the other hand, if you do not see even slight improvements in the areas your fitness program has concentrated on, it is time to reevaluate your approach. Make certain you are following all guidelines suggested in this book. Refer to the specific chapters on each fitness component and make workout adjustments. Continue to regularly reassess until you

reach your goals. Periodically (for example, yearly) perform the assessments to make certain you are not slipping, to motivate and reward your hard work, and to remind yourself how far you have come.

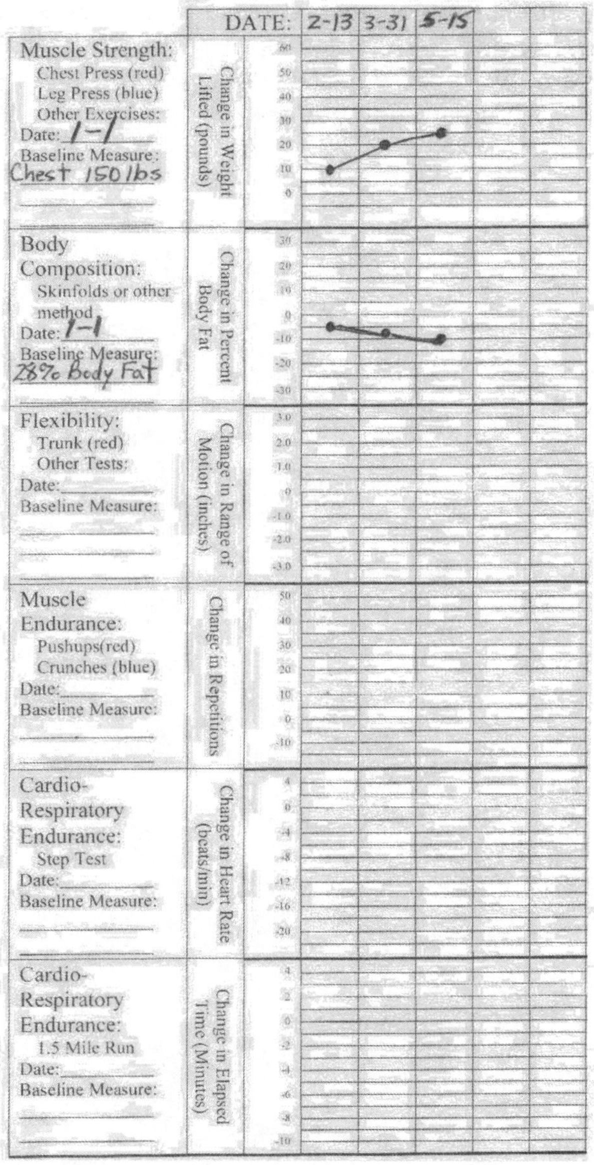

Figure 3.12: Sample Progression Chart

SUMMARY

Measurement and evaluation are very important in our everyday lives. How many miles to the gallon of gasoline do we get? Which product is the better buy? How does a professor rate as a teacher? We continuously measure and evaluate various facets of our daily living. Through the use of objective physical fitness tests you can evaluate your own level of physical fitness and/or how effective your training program has been. The tests discussed in this chapter are all easily administered and provide useful ratings of the physical fitness of men and women. The success of the testing program, however, depends on careful and accurate administration of the tests.

Testing should not dominate your exercise program, but it can be a worthwhile motivator to greater effort and to regular, desirable exercise habits. It is also natural to be curious about how you compare with others. The tables in this chapter allow you to see where you stand based on your test results and will give you greater insight into your physical strengths and weaknesses. Use this information to develop your individualized physical fitness program. The following chapters examine the benefits and discuss the training specifics for improving and maintaining optimal cardiorespiratory endurance, muscular strength and endurance, flexibility, and body composition.

The Basic Principles of Exercise

This chapter discusses the foundational concepts that need to be considered when developing a personalized exercise program. In recent years advances in exercise and sports science have led to the development of safe and effective guidelines for exercise prescription. We now know that exercise programs must be designed around each individual. Also, we recognize that any physical fitness program is more than just jogging or weight lifting. An effective physical fitness exercise program must involve a balance of training for cardiorespiratory endurance, muscular strength and endurance, flexibility, and body composition.

Without a clear understanding of the basic principles of exercise, it would be easy to embark on a sporadic, unsafe, and ineffective training program. The result could be unnecessary soreness, frustration, discouragement, and possibly injury. The basic exercise principles presented here apply equally well to men and women regardless of age or physical condition. Proper application of these principles will allow you to design and/or adapt your exercise program to suit your changing physical needs or fitness goals as you go through life. Gaining an understanding of the basic principles of exercise is a crucial first step towards adopting physical fitness as a way of life.

Carefully read the following questions and after each one formulate the answer in your mind. If you don't know the answer, then read the chapter with the intent of finding the answer. If you did answer the question, then read to make sure your answer is correct and not a misconception you have about how to put together an exercise program.

- Why is it important to design the exercise program based on your own individual capabilities?
- Is it necessary to push the limits of your physical capability in order to gain benefits from your exercise program?
- Why should the exercise program you design take into account your personal physical fitness goals?
- Once you achieve your personal fitness goals, what do you need to do to maintain your level of physical fitness?
- What are the basic elements of a well-constructed workout session?

WHAT IS THE PREMISE BEHIND THE "INDIVIDUALITY PRINCIPLE"?

According to the **individuality principle**, no one program can be designed to accommodate everyone because we all differ in initial fitness levels, physical attributes, physical limitations, and training goals. Just because we are all interested in having healthy cardiorespiratory systems does not mean that everyone can just go out and perform the same training program. Even the popular cable television shows and exercise DVD's that you think are de-

> **INDIVIDUALITY PRINCIPLE:**
> A basic training principle that states an exercise program should be designed around each person's weaknesses/strengths and/or fitness priorities.

signed for everyone warn that you should exercise at your own pace and perform only those movements within your capabilities. Another analogy would be to say that anyone interested in getting stronger should start a training program by performing the bench press with 150 pounds. This would be too light for some, just right for a few, and crushingly heavy to others.

i start everyone at this weight. You can do it!

PERSONAL TRAINER

There is no one set program that works for everyone. The best programs are designed around your strengths and weaknesses.

The purpose of undergoing the various fitness assessments outlined in Chapter 3 was to help you ascertain your current fitness level and increase your awareness of which fitness component needs improvement. Before embarking on a new training program or changing your current one, you should assess your current fitness level and write down your reasons for starting or continuing an exercise program. Once you have written down your reasons for exercising, prioritize them. Armed with your testing results and priority list, you can begin to individualize your training by designing a program that meets your specific fitness goals. Following the individuality principle will not only help you start a successful

A WAY OF LIFE

Write down your reasons for exercising and prioritize them. Doing so will help you individualize your program and improve the odds of its long-term success.

exercise program but it will also serve to help you maintain a lifelong fitness program. An individual's life is always in a state of flux and likewise so should the exercise program. Limitations due to injury and illness or changes in your fitness goals will require you to routinely reassess your training program. Designing or upgrading a program in this fashion will help enhance its effectiveness and thus provide great positive reinforcement for you to continue making exercise an ongoing part of your life.

WHY IS THE "OVERLOAD PRINCIPLE" CRUCIAL TO THE SUCCESS OF AN EXERCISE PROGRAM?

In order to improve physical fitness, you must ask your body to do something it is not used to doing on a regular basis. The body is not challenged by activities to which it is accustomed and as a result, does not adapt. Therefore, a properly designed training program must incorporate regular training that observes the **overload principle**. Fortunately, meeting the physical demands of the overload principle

OVERLOAD PRINCIPLE:
A basic training principle that states an activity must physically challenge the body beyond what is accustomed to in order to get it to adapt.

A WAY OF LIFE

Meeting the physical demands of the overload principle doesn't mean that your workouts have to be punishing or exhaustive.

doesn't mean that your workouts have to be punishing or exhaustive. The requirements of the overload principle are met by manipulating three training variables: intensity, frequency, and duration. These three variables can be adjusted to control the physical challenge imposed by your fitness program. A brief discussion of each follows.

Table 4.1. Training Variables Associated With the Overload Principle

- Intensity—How hard?
- Duration—How long?
- Frequency—How often?

What is "intensity" of training?

Intensity refers to how difficult the training is. The higher the intensity, the more strenuous you perceive the training to be. The intensity of

> **INTENSITY:**
> A training variable associated with the overload principle that refers to how physically challenging the training is.

a training program is judged differently depending upon the nature of the exercise (see Figure 4.1). For example, the intensity of a cardiorespiratory (i.e. aerobic) training program is generally based on **exercise heart rate**. The higher the heart rate the more intense the workout. For strength training the intensity is based on the amount of weight lifted. The intensity for each flexibility exercise is based on the degree of discomfort experienced while stretching. Specifics on intensity for each type of training will be discussed in the following chapters.

> **EXERCISE HEART RATE:**
> The pulse rate or beats per minute the heart is achieving during exercise. It is an indication of the intensity of aerobic exercise.

Figure 4.1: Intensity of Exercise

What does "duration" refer to?

Duration refers to the length of time the body is actually being overloaded during a

> **DURATION:**
> A training variable associated with the overload principle that denotes the length of the workout session.

training workout. The duration of a workout varies depending upon the type of exercise being performed (see Figure 4.2). Cardiorespi-

Figure 4.2: Duration of Exercise

ratory exercise is usually continuous activity that is performed for 20 to 60 minutes. The duration of a strength training workout is dictated by the number of specific muscle exercises performed and the amount of rest taken in between each. For flexibility the duration is determined by the amount of time the stretch is held and the total number of stretches performed. Specifics on the duration required for each type of training will be discussed in subsequent chapters.

What is meant by "frequency" of training?

Frequency refers to the number of times (usually on a per week basis) that you work out. As with intensity and duration, the frequency of training varies with the type of train-

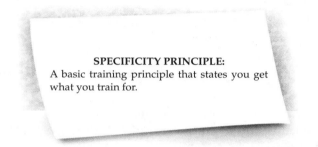

> **FREQUENCY:**
> A training variable associated with the overload principle that refers to the number of times (usually on a per week basis) training is performed.

ing and the goals of your fitness program (see Figure 4.3). Cardiorespiratory training is usually performed 3 to 5 times per week while strength training is performed 2 to 3 times per week. Flexibility training can be performed seven times per week. Again, specifics

Figure 4.3: Frequency of Exercise

on the frequency for each type of exercise will be discussed in the following chapters.

As already stated adjusting one, two or all three of these variables (i.e. intensity, duration, frequency) will affect the training overload. Learning how to manipulate these training variables will enable you to adapt your training based on your changing personal fitness goals as you go through life.

WHY IS IT IMPORTANT TO OBSERVE THE "SPECIFICITY PRINCIPLE"?

The **specificity principle** states that the body adapts in a very specific manner to the demands placed upon it by training. The adaptations the body makes are biomechanically, anatomically, and physiologically specific to the type of training performed. In other words, the changes the body undergoes are specific to

> **SPECIFICITY PRINCIPLE:**
> A basic training principle that states you get what you train for.

body positioning while exercising, the mode of exercise (i.e. running, swimming, biking, etc.), the joint angles and range of motion used during training, the muscles involved, and the nature (i.e. speed and duration) of the movements performed during training. For example, running does little to improve your performance in biking even though you are using many of the same muscles. Why, you may ask? The reason is because of differences in biomechanical specificity. The muscles are being used differently in the two activities. In running the muscles are carrying body weight and are moving forward and backward in rhythmic strides that move the body forward. In biking the leg muscles are not supporting body weight and rotational movements are used to push/pull on the pedals that provide forward propulsion.

Another application of the specificity principle is that while running causes large increases in the muscular endurance of the leg muscles, the anatomical specificity of run training causes little improvement in upper body muscular endurance. In a similar manner, exclusively weight training the upper body muscles will not cause any strength improvements in the leg muscles or vice versa.

I never miss an arm workout.

Training adaptations are specific and limited to the parts of the body that are worked regularly.

Physiological specificity tells us that walking or jogging for improved cardiorespiratory and muscular endurance does little to cause changes in leg muscle strength. Again, why may you ask? The physiologic demands placed upon the leg muscles during endurance training are different from those of strength training. With endurance training the muscles are subjected to repetitive, relatively low intensity muscle contractions that are performed continuously for 20 to 60 minutes. Conversely, in strength training the muscles are subjected to lift heavy weights for a few repetitions and then allowed to rest and recover before beginning again. In a similar example, endurance run training does not increase sprinting ability. Again, despite the fact that the same muscles are being used, physiological specificity dictates that since the speed with which a muscle contracts and the energy requirements are dif-ferent between endurance training and sprint training, the adaptations elicited by each will be different.

The specificity principle is one reason why elite athletes must concentrate on one sport or activity. Their program must be designed to elicit the sport-specific adaptations that will enhance all aspects of performance in their sport. This explains why no one athlete can dominate in all sports. Although there are great heptathletes and decathletes, none reach the levels of sport performance that the single event specialists do. Obviously no one training program could adequately prepare an athlete for the variety of demands required by the different sports.

However, training for overall physical fitness is much different than training for the specialized demands of sport participation. A general fitness training program should be designed to improve or at least maintain all the components of physical fitness. As a result, keep in mind the importance of participating in a balanced fitness program with an emphasis on fitness components that demonstrate a weakness. For example, if your fitness goal is to improve your muscle strength, then priori-

A WAY OF LIFE

A general fitness training program should be designed to at least maintain all the components of physical fitness. As a result, keep in mind the importance of participating in a balanced fitness program with an emphasis on fitness components that demonstrate a weakness

tize your training accordingly. This does not mean that you don't train for cardiorespiratory endurance but that you spend more of your training time working on muscle strength and less on cardiorespiratory endurance. Simply changing the order in which you train can be enough. In other words, training for strength before you go out for a run would be a way of prioritizing your training for the greatest improvements in strength. A word of warning, you would not want to prioritize your training so much as to stop training for the other fitness components (see Reversibility Principle). Training programs designed with the specificity principle in mind ensure that you to get the most from your exercise program and enable you to adapt your program whenever your fitness priorities change.

WHAT'S THE IMPORTANCE OF OBSERVING THE "REVERSIBILITY PRINCIPLE"?

Regular exercise allows you to improve or maintain your fitness capabilities. But, if your workouts are sporadic or stop altogether, your fitness level will drop to a level that only meets your current physical demands of daily living. Simply stated the **reversibility principle** says that if you don't use it, you lose it. If you stop

REVERSIBILITY PRINICPLE:
A basic training principle that states if you don't continue to use it, you lose it.

training, you will begin to lose the training adaptations you worked so hard for. This is why we say "fitness is for life". Training is not something you do 3 months out of the year in

order to get ready for swimsuit weather. It is something you do year round! Although your reasons for training will certainly change at dif-

A WAY OF LIFE

Because of the reversibility principle, it is important to understand that leading an active lifestyle, which includes regular exercise, is a lifelong venture.

ferent times of the year and as you go through life, it is critical that you adapt your training program without interrupting its regularity. Knowledge of the four basic training principles (i.e. overload, individuality, specificity, and reversibility) will help you effectively adapt your training and enable you to enjoy the benefits of a lifelong exercise program.

SUMMARY

Most people know the virtues of physical fitness, yet many of these same people do not start or maintain a regular fitness program. The primary reason for this is not knowing how to put an exercise program together. In this chapter we discussed the four basic training principles of program design and gave practical examples of each. You can be as creative and individual in your program design as you want to be as long as you take into consideration the overload, specificity, individuality, and reversibility training principles. In doing so your program is guaranteed to be effective.

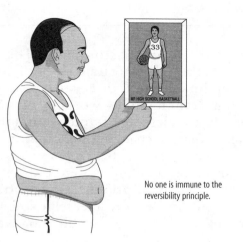

No one is immune to the reversibility principle.

5 The Anatomy of a Workout

As we stated at the beginning of Chapter 1, this book is about *you*. Exercise professionals know full well that you, along with a vast number of your fellow human beings, may not be living a fitness-oriented lifestyle mainly because of time constraints mixed with confusion about your options. This chapter is devoted to helping you design your exercise session so that you reach your goals in the most time-efficient manner possible. This is where you begin to take the responsibility to develop a plan that works for you. This is where you begin to establish a lifelong fitness philosophy. Perhaps your immediate goal is to get a good grade in class. Hopefully, after the class, you will continue your fitness lifestyle even though no more rewarding grades will be coming. Your fitness well-being is more than a 10 to 16 week class: it is for a lifetime

Read the following questions and after each one formulate the answer in your mind. If you don't know the answer, then read the chapter with the intent of finding the answer. If you did answer the question, then read to make sure your answer is correct and not a misconception you have about how to design a workout session.

- What are the basic elements of a workout?
- How should I start each workout session?
- How should I end each workout session?
- Do workouts for the various physical fitness components all begin and end the same way?

- How do I know I'm ready for the more vigorous conditioning portion of my workout?
- Is it safe to eliminate any portions of a workout session?

WHAT ARE THE BASIC ELEMENTS OF A WORKOUT?

Very few people have the ability, the time and lifestyle, or the desire to achieve the level of physical fitness of an Olympic competitor. Still, anyone who wishes to improve their fitness potential, albeit on a more realistic level, can certainly do so. The key to improving physical fitness is working out on a regular basis. The following sections discuss the basic elements of a workout session (i.e. the warm-up, the conditioning period, the cool-down). These basic elements should be a part of everyone's workout whether an Olympic-caliber athlete or someone simply wanting to make physical fitness a way of life.

A WAY OF LIFE

The basic elements of a workout are the warm-up, the conditioning period, and the cool-down.

WHY WARM-UP?

When you watch children head outside for recess do you see them prepare for their activity by intentionally moving from a slow pace to a gradually increasing pace? Do you see them stop and stretch before they jump on the monkey bars? Of course not! They simply make a mad dash for their favorite activity and go at it with all they've got. In a similar manner, when they know it's time for the bell to ring, do they gradually slow their activity and finish with a stretching session before heading back inside? Heck no, they drag out their play as long as possible, finally heading inside only to stand in line for a drink at the water fountain.

Kids can get away with this free-form, stop-start style of active movement. However for safety and comfort, adults need to consider a more formatted and thoughtful approach to exercising. In order to prepare our bodies for vigorous movement, a **warm-up** of some kind is recommended. The goal of the warm-up is to progressively increase your heart and breathing rates from resting levels to those encountered during exercise. In other words, the warm-up allows the body to ramp up rather than make the big jump from rest to vigorous exercise. The warm-up helps prepare the body for exercise by delivering more blood and oxygen to the muscles that are about to be used. Sending warm blood to the muscles physically increases the temperature of the muscles, thus the name warm-up. Increasing the temperature of muscles makes them more elastic and promotes ease of movement.

> **WARM-UP:**
> The beginning element of a workout that prepares your body for more vigorous exercise. The warm-up period generally consists of a toned-down, reduced-intensity version of your chosen activity.

Many individuals think that stretching before exercise constitutes the warm-up. However, this is a misconception. While stretching can be incorporated into the warm-up, by itself it is not a warm-up. The act of stretching does nothing to increase blood flow to the muscles that are about to be exercised and as a result, does not increase muscle temperature. This misconception grew from the fact that athletes are many times seen stretching prior to compe-

tition. However, what most people don't realize is that the athletes have actually already performed some form of physical activity prior to stretching. In other words, they have already increased their body temperatures and are taking advantage of the increased muscle temperature to increase their range of motion prior to competition.

A WAY OF LIFE

Do not confuse stretching with warming-up. The act of stretching in and of itself does little to increase muscle temperature.

The warm-up can be either a formal period of time with specific tasks to perform or a more random, adjust-as-you-go period. The warm-up for a resistance training workout may be slightly different from that of a cardiorespiratory endurance workout. With these variables in mind, let's look at suggested warm-ups for the different fitness components.

How Should I Warm-up for Cardiorespiratory Endurance Training?

Those of us who grew up in the last century may remember beginning our physical education classes with stretches followed by vigorous activities. We now know that this is not the best sequence of events when preparing for movement. Instead, spend 3 to 5 minutes prior to beginning your conditioning period performing a toned-down, reduced-intensity version of your chosen activity. For example, before a run start with a brisk walk or a slow jog. You can increase your pace each minute, gradually increasing the intensity until you are in your target heart rate range (see Chapter 6). You also should be breathing more heavily and have broken a sweat. At this point you are ready for your conditioning period.

However, if you feel rather tight in a particular muscle group during this warm-up, now would be the point where you stop and perform a static stretch for that muscle group (see Chapter 8). Each stretch will require 20 or more seconds to perform. Since you will no longer be moving, your heart rate will begin to decline (the fitter you are, the more rapidly this decline will take place). Therefore, before you enter the conditioning period of your workout perform an additional 'mini-warm-up' to elevate your heart and breathing rates once again.

Can I Take A Less Regimented Warm-up for Cardiorespiratory Endurance Training?

As you become more experienced in your workouts, you may be able to 'feel' your way through a warm-up. Pay careful attention to your body as you progressively reach that point where your heart and breathing rates are elevated, you are sweating and feeling 'loose'. Some people reach that point much sooner than others. It may require trial and error to find your perfect warm-up. There also may be some days where your 'regular' warm-up is inadequate. One example of this is when the weather turns frigid, extending the length of time before you are ready to work at a moderately vigorous intensity.

How Should I Warm-up for Resistance Training?

Since elevating your heart rate into a target range is not a main goal of resistance training you would think that your warm-up would be entirely different from the ones used for cardiorespiratory endurance training. This is not necessarily so. Weightlifting will be much more comfortable if your muscles and connective tissues are 'warm' when you begin your first set. If you are in a gym and have access to cardiorespiratory endurance equipment such as treadmills or stationary bikes use them at a low intensity level for 3 to 5 minutes. If there is no equipment you can jog in place or step up and down on stairs. Make sure to involve your arms if you will be performing strength exercises for your upper body. Try swinging, pressing or pumping motions.

Since resistance training exercises typically are performed in a full range of motion, you may not need formal stretching exercises before you begin your weight lifting. However, if you feel especially tight in a particular muscle group following your low intensity activity, now would be the point where you stop and perform a static stretch for that muscle group (see Chapter 8). Each stretch should be held for at least 20 or more seconds. Do not worry about repeating a 'mini-warm-up' after you stretch since an elevated heart rate is not important in resistance training.

A different type of warm-up for resistance training involves performing a light preliminary set of each exercise before beginning the conditioning period where overloading the muscles occurs. Choose a weight that is 50 percent of your normal conditioning weight and perform 15 to 20 repetitions with good form. Since the weight will feel relatively light, you may find yourself tempted to rush through the moves: resist that temptation. Regardless of the load, controlled movements do a better job getting your mind-body connection in place for your subsequent heavier weight. It also makes sense safety-wise to keep movements controlled and sharp.

How Should I Warm-up To Prepare For Flexibility Training?

If you always keep in mind the very important guideline for stretching that suggests you move only to a position of slight discomfort and not pain, then you can stretch anytime you want (see Chapter 8). However, you will benefit more from a stretching session if your muscles and connective tissues are properly warmed up. Raising the temperature of the muscles helps make them more pliable, more capable of a full range of motion at the joints. Follow the same type of active 3 to 5 minute warm-up as was discussed for both cardiorespiratory endurance and resistance training. The goal is not necessarily to increase your heart and breathing rates, so don't worry about sustaining those following the warm-up. As was the case for the resistance training warm-up, perform movements that involve the muscle groups you are about to stretch.

WHAT IS THE CONDITIONING PERIOD?

After the warm-up, you are ready for the main **conditioning period** of your workout. This is the period of time in which the body is vigorously worked. The conditioning period can consist of any physically challenging activity as long as the frequency, intensity, and duration are sufficient to cause a training response (see Overload Principle, Chapter 4). Activities such as walking, running, bicycling, swimming, aerobics, calisthenics, resistance

> **CONDITIONING PERIOD:**
> The portion of a workout in which the body is vigorously exercised. The conditioning period can consist of any physically challenging activity as long as the frequency, intensity, and duration are sufficient to cause a training response.

training, interval training, and circuit training are all possible training activities. Combinations of activities can also be used during the conditioning segment. For example, you could perform both biking and running or weight training and jogging into a single workout session. This is known as **cross training** and adds variety and enjoyment to your workout. On

> **CROSS TRAINING:**
> A type of training that involves performing different modes of exercise.

some days, vigorous participation in your favorite sport may be used as the conditioning activity. The key is to make sure your intensity of training is sufficient to stimulate your body to adapt. In the following chapters, we examine the training intensities required for the various modes of exercise. One consideration to keep in mind concerning exercise intensity is how well you recover from your workout. One hour after your exercise session you should feel no adverse affects. If you experience fatigue that lingers on for a few hours, this is your body telling you to back off a little during your next workout. Disregard the old

adage "No pain, no gain!" It is poor advice when it comes to developing physical fitness.

The remainder of this book goes into detail about the conditioning period requirements for improving the various components of physical fitness. You will need this information to appropriately design your conditioning period so that your fitness goals can be achieved.

WHAT IS THE COOL-DOWN?

The **cool-down** is the tapering-off of activity upon completion of the vigorous conditioning period. The activities performed during the cool-down vary depending upon the type of activity used in the preceding conditioning period. For example, after strength training, the

> **COOL-DOWN:**
> The last element of a workout consisting of a tapering-off in exercise intensity. The cool-down should include light general-type activity along with stretching exercises.

cool-down may consist of slow and controlled movements mimicking those used in training combined with stretching. On the other hand, a cool-down segment is not normally needed after flexibility training.

For cardiorespiratory training, the cool-down may be a continuation of activity at a progressively lower intensity. The cool-down prevents pooling of blood in the extremities and enables the cardiorespiratory system to slowly return to resting levels. The light muscle activity of the cool-down assists in returning blood from the extremities back to the heart. If you end a cardiorespiratory workout abruptly, your heart will continue to send extra blood to the muscles for a few minutes. Since the muscles are no longer contracting and helping to propel the blood back to the heart, blood pools in the extremities. In some cases the blood pooling can cause dizziness and fainting after a workout. Generally, a 5 to 10 minute cool-down period is sufficient to help the body return back to near resting conditions. For most participants, the heart rate at the end of the cool-down should be below 100 beats per minute.

It is recommended that stretching be performed towards the end of the cool-down segment. Stretching at the end of the workout has been shown to be effective particularly since it is at this time that the muscle is warm and pliable. The increased muscle elasticity allows for a greater range of motion about the joints and thus greater potential for improvements in flexibility.

SUMMARY

We examined the three components of a workout and the reasoning behind these. Remember that the conditioning segment is the foundation of any exercise program and can involve any activity or group of activities that stimulate and develop the various components of fitness. Keep in mind the importance of engaging in light muscular activity and stretching exercises during the warm-up and cool-down.

Well-designed workout sessions are safe, time effective. The three components of a workout can be thought of as the skeleton on which to build any exercise program, regardless of the particular physical fitness components you have set as your goals. The ensuing chapters will fill in the details as to how to structure the conditioning component of the workout sessions so you can achieve any fitness goal. In a sense, when you complete this book, you will become your own personal trainer and will be able to adjust your program accordingly as your fitness goals change throughout your lifetime.

6 Improving Cardiorespiratory Endurance

What if you had to name the most important muscle in your body? Which one would you choose? If you said the heart you would be correct: if the heart is not functioning optimally the rest of the body suffers. This chapter covers the specifics of how to plan a program for developing and maintaining **cardiorespiratory endurance**. Such a program conditions the heart, lungs, and blood vessels and improves their ability to deliver oxygen to the muscle tissue. Exercise programs involving

> **CARDIORESPIRATORY ENDURANCE:**
> The fitness component describing a high level of conditioning of the heart, lungs, and blood vessels and their ability to deliver oxygen to the muscle tissue.

the large muscle groups in continuous and rhythmic movements that are moderately hard in intensity will provide significant improvements in cardiorespiratory endurance. Widely practiced modes include walking, running, swimming, biking, rowing, cross-country skiing, jumping rope, and various 'cardio' equipment including elliptical trainers and stair climbers.

This chapter describes in detail how to design a cardiorespiratory endurance exercise program that meets the standards for mode, intensity, duration, and frequency currently endorsed by scientific research. You will then be able to choose an activity and design a program around these guidelines that will insure a safe, effective workout. We offer descriptions of the various cardiorespiratory endurance activities that you can choose from. Each activity offers something unique. We highly recommend trying as many activities as possible in order to achieve your fitness goals.

Read the following questions and after each one formulate the answer in your mind. If you don't know the answer, then read the chapter with the intent of finding the answer. If you did answer the question, then read to make sure your answer is correct and not a misconception you have about cardiorespiratory endurance training.

- Why should I spend time performing aerobic forms of exercise?
- How intensely should I perform a cardiorespiratory endurance activity?
- Is one aerobic activity superior to all the others?
- Do I have to perform my cardiorespiratory endurance exercise for a long period of time or can I break it into smaller chunks of time?

WHAT ARE THE BENEFITS OF CARDIORESPIRATORY EXERCISE?

The benefits of cardiorespiratory endurance exercise are numerous, paramount of which is the reduction of risk for cardiovascular disease and premature death. Cardiorespiratory endurance exercise is also referred to as **aerobic exercise** since oxygen must be continuously delivered to the working muscles. We will use the terms 'cardiorespiratory endurance exercise' and 'aerobic exercise' inter-

AEROBIC EXERCISE:
A type of exercise that works large muscles of the body and requires delivery of oxygen to the working muscles. This form of exercise is synonymous with cardiorespiratory endurance exercise.

changeably. Aerobic workouts demand high levels of oxygen and vigorously stimulate the heart and lungs. The pumping ability of the heart, breathing capacity of the lungs, and

usage of energy within the trained skeletal muscles are all enhanced. Each cell needs a ready supply of oxygen and food, while carbon dioxide and other waste products must be carried away. Exercise facilitates these tasks by improving the circulatory system's (the heart and blood vessels) ability to circulate the blood throughout the body. Additionally, the respiratory system (the lungs and air passages) becomes better at removing carbon dioxide and replacing it with fresh oxygen.

The exercised heart, lungs and muscles gradually function at a higher level both during physical exertion as well as at rest. These improvements are referred to as the **training effect**. The training effect of cardiorespiratory exercise manifests itself in many ways. For example, the **cardiac output** at rest is approximately the same for those who exercise regularly as for those who do not. While there is no

TRAINING EFFECT:
Gradual improvements to the exercised heart, lungs and muscles which allow them to function at a higher level both during physical exertion as well as at rest.

change in cardiac output after a period of endurance-type training (six to eight weeks) there is generally a reduction in the resting heart

CARDIAC OUTPUT:
The amount of blood pumped per minute by the heart.

rate. The heart pumps more blood with each beat and does not have to beat as often to supply the body with blood. *It has become a more effective pump*. In addition, the slower heart

rate provides a greater rest for the heart between beats. The magnitude of this decrease in resting heart rate is dependent not only on the length of time you have been training but also on the intensity and amount of training. Let's say that after a couple of months of exercise training you were able to lower your average per-minute resting heart rate by 10 beats. This would mean that your heart is beating 14,400 fewer times a day. A relatively slow heart rate coupled with the greater volume of blood pumped per beat make for an efficient circulatory system.

During vigorous activity, the exercising muscles must use increased amounts of oxygen to make energy. The maximum effort you can exert over a prolonged period of time is limited by your ability to deliver oxygen to the active tissues. **Aerobic capacity** is the greatest amount of oxygen that you can consume per minute and is a functional measure of your cardiorespiratory endurance. Regular cardiorespiratory exer-

> **AEROBIC CAPACITY/ VO$_2$ MAX:**
> The greatest amount of oxygen that your body can consume on a per minute basis during exercise. It is synonymous with maximal oxygen consumption or VO2max and is a functional measure of your cardiorespiratory endurance.

cise will produce a training effect that can increase your aerobic capacity by as much as 20 to 30 percent. The precise amount of increase depends on your pre-training status and on the intensity and duration of your training program.

A WAY OF LIFE

Cross-country skiers historically are the athletes with the highest levels of VO$_2$ max. Their sport requires extremely rigorous amounts of work from all the major muscle groups.

You might ask, why do I need a higher aerobic capacity? Theoretically, a higher aerobic capacity indicates an increased ability of the heart to pump oxygen-rich blood and of the muscle cells to take up oxygen and use it for energy production. Maintaining an optimal aerobic capacity improves energy levels for most activities and provides for a healthy cardiovascular system.

A WAY OF LIFE

Optimizing your aerobic capacity improves your energy levels for most activities.

Aerobic capacity gradually declines with age regardless of one's training status. Shortly after you reach adulthood (age 18 to 21) your aerobic capacity begins to decline. However, the decrease is greater in inactive and overweight people and in those who have developed diseases of the heart and lungs.

Another training effect of aerobic exercise is the increased capacity of the exercising muscles to generate energy by using oxygen. Two key adaptations within the muscle cell contribute to this improved capacity. First, there is an increase in the number, size, and membrane surface area of the **mitochondria**. Mitochondria are specialized compartments in the cell.

> **MITOCHONDRIA:**
> Specialized compartments in the cell containing the enzymes necessary for making the energy needed for muscular contraction. Mitochondria are the so-called "powerhouses" of the cell where energy is created.

These compartments contain the enzymes necessary for making the energy needed for muscular contraction. Mitochondria are the so-called "powerhouses" of the cell where energy is created. Second, training causes increases in the enzymes responsible for the creation of

A WAY OF LIFE

Mitochondria are the so-called "powerhouses" of the cell where energy is created. Aerobic training causes those mitochondria to increase in number, size, and membrane surface.

aerobic energy in the muscle. In short, with increased numbers of powerhouses (mitochondria) and a corresponding increase in enzymes (compounds that accelerate the speed of chemical reactions), the trained muscle is able to produce greater amounts of energy and sustain higher levels of physical activity or performance.

Several studies have indicated that active people tend to have lower resting blood pressures than most sedentary people. Whether lowered blood pressure is a training effect of exercise alone is still questionable. When blood pressure is normal, vigorous endurance-type exercise has little if any effect on lowering blood pressure any further. For people who already have serious complications related to high blood pressure, the ability of exercise alone to lower blood pressure may be limited. However, the combination of an altered diet, medication, and exercise appears to be a promising approach to controlling this major risk factor of heart disease.

The evidence of the effects of exercise on the concentration levels of fat substances, or lipids, in the blood is encouraging. Cholesterol, triglycerides, low-density lipoproteins and high-density lipoproteins are the blood lipids most often studied in heart disease research. People who are active and who adhere to sound nutritional practices tend to have a more favorable blood lipid profile, one that reduces their risk for heart disease.

Luckily the non-stop activities that benefit our heart and lungs also help achieve and maintain ideal body composition by requiring steady amounts of energy. Many studies have shown that body fat can be reduced with regular vigorous training, particularly when combined with sensible eating. It appears that exercise plays an even more critical role when it comes to the notoriously difficult task of maintaining ideal body fat levels following weight loss. You may notice that people who possess high levels of physical fitness are seldom overweight. A strong, lean physique is virtually impossible with dieting alone and must come from the addition of a well-rounded exercise program.

The bones and muscles repetitively stressed during exercise benefit as well. Loss of bone mineral content (**osteoporosis**) is slowed

or prevented, and muscles improve their endurance. **Weight-bearing exercise** such as running or walking seem to contribute to the

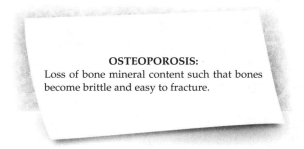

OSTEOPOROSIS:
Loss of bone mineral content such that bones become brittle and easy to fracture.

strengthening of bones more effectively than non-weight-bearing exercise forms such as biking or swimming. Because of this, savvy bikers and swimmers add resistance training to their workout plan to adequately stress the bones.

WEIGHT-BEARING EXERCISE:
Endurance activities where one or both feet maintain contact with the ground and support the body.

Many enjoyable competitive sports build on cardiorespiratory endurance activities. Competitive athletes first lay down a good level of aerobic fitness and then proceed to learn the skills and techniques of more advanced pursuits. Triathletes, marathon runners, and bike racers are a few examples of competitive athletes who rely on advanced levels of cardiorespiratory endurance in order to be successful.

Ask a group of physically fit individuals if they find aerobic training to be uplifting and many will respond that they experience an emotional high during and/or shortly after a workout (sometimes referred to as a 'runner's high'). Research studies have examined this exercise-induced increase in **endorphins**, substances produced in the pituitary gland, brain, and other tissues. These endorphins were

ENDORPHINS:
Substances produced in the pituitary gland, brain, and other tissues said to have morphine-like qualities in reducing pain and producing a euphoric state during exercise.

found to have morphine-like qualities in reducing pain and producing a euphoric state. Not all aerobic exercisers experience this 'high', however. There are some limitations with these studies, and additional research is needed to fully comprehend the role of endorphins in producing this exercise-induced euphoria.

A WAY OF LIFE

Many aerobic exercise participants experience an emotional 'high' during and following a workout. Don't think there is something wrong if you personally do not feel this phenomenon as it is truly not universal.

The following section discusses how to apply the four training specifics, type (mode), intensity, duration, and frequency, to cardiorespiratory endurance training. Proper application of these four factors will assure that you begin an exercise program that is well within your present health and physical capabilities

yet will challenge you sufficiently to reach your fitness goals. As you begin to see the results of your training, you may surprise yourself by replacing the question "What workout do I *have* to do?" with "What workout do I *get* to do?"

WHAT ARE THE TRAINING SPECIFICS REGARDING CARDIORESPIRATORY EXERCISE?

What Type of Exercise Should I Perform?

Exercises that utilize the large muscle groups and are rhythmic and continuous are recommended for improving and maintaining cardiorespiratory endurance. Aerobic exercise relies on the oxygen energy systems to fuel these activities that continue for long periods of time. Remember: because these activities require large amounts of energy, they are also recommended for improving and maintaining ideal body composition. The intensity level of your chosen activity must be high enough to produce a training effect for your circulatory and respiratory systems. When choosing an activity you should realize that those low in intensity and short in duration produce low levels of improvement. In fact, they may not result in any fitness improvements at all. The relative values of various activities for improving physical fitness depend on the physiological intensity required. Thus, start/stop sports of lower intensities like golf, bowling, archery, and softball do little to develop or maintain cardiorespiratory endurance. These activities are great fun and may contribute to health maintenance, but they do not require enough physical effort from your cardiorespiratory system for the necessary physiological stimulus and overload.

A WAY OF LIFE

Rhythmic, continuous exercise using the large muscle groups make up an aerobic exercise workout.

A popular choice for many beginners is a walking or run/walk program, an activity that comes naturally and requires only a good pair of shoes and safe place to walk. By following the suggestions regarding intensity, duration, and frequency discussed further on, even those possessing low fitness levels or musculoskeletal weaknesses can progress safely.

It seems that every few years a fresh and unique type of cardiorespiratory exercise is introduced, attracting new exercisers and experienced fitness enthusiasts alike. Sometimes these activities are hybrids of already existing modes. This is particularly true in the area of group exercise or aerobics classes. In order to keep participants motivated enough to continue attending a class, a new twist or entirely new form is introduced. This is fine as long as all of the principles of training continue to be adhered to. Consider the evolution of choreographed aerobic dance in the 1970s to the free form high impact and low impact **aerobics** of the 1980s all the way to step classes and spinning classes of the 1990s.

AEROBICS:
A variety of vigorous exercise routines and activities performed to music.

The 'menu' of cardiorespiratory activity choices today also includes biking, swimming, elliptical machines and 'cross-trainers', dance and step aerobics, water aerobics and water running, stair-climbing, rowing, cross country skiing, jumping rope, and in-line skating. These activities can stand on their own as your chosen exercise mode. Additionally, two or more can be combined for 'cross training' either on separate days or within the same workout. As long as your exercise intensity stays in your '**target heart rate range**' (see 'Intensity') with continuous-type exertions you can achieve your cardiorespiratory endurance goals. By cross training you add variety, which can improve your adherence to an exercise program. You also are able to utilize many different muscle groups and joint angles to help achieve balanced fitness. Aerobic activities can be categorized either as weight-bearing exer-

cise, where one or both feet maintain contact with the ground and support the body, or as non-weight bearing where the exerciser is seated or buoyed by water. Additionally, cardiorespiratory exercise is categorized as either **non-impact** (impact is not transferred from one foot to the other), **low impact** (one foot always maintains contact with the exercise surface), **high impact** (at some point both feet are off the exercise surface), or a combination of impacts. Choosing from different categories may mini-

NON-IMPACT EXERCISE:
Endurance activities where impact is not transferred from foot to foot and includes non-weight bearing exercise.

LOW IMPACT EXERCISE:
Endurance activities where one foot always maintains contact with the exercise surface.

HIGH IMPACT EXERCISE:
Endurance activities where both feet are off the exercise surface at one point or another.

mize the chance for overuse injuries. Following is a list categorizing the most common aerobic activities to help you choose the workout most appropriate for you.

- Weight-bearing + low impact: walking, low impact aerobics, cross country skiing, stair -climbing, step aerobics (excluding jumps and hops), elliptical training, in-line skating
- Weight-bearing + high impact: running, high impact aerobics, jumping rope
- Non-weight bearing: swimming, biking, rowing, deep water running

Is Working Out At Home Better Than Training At A Fitness Center?

It would be safe to guess that anyone who exercises on a regular basis has weighed the benefits and drawbacks of belonging to a commercial fitness center versus creating a home workout center. While a fitness membership offers an unrivaled variety of equipment, classes, and amenities along with a unique social atmosphere, owning one or more pieces of cardiorespiratory exercise equipment may be a better fit for your life. Home equipment not only provides an excellent stimulus for cardiorespiratory conditioning but adds conve-

nience (and therefore motivation) to an exercise program as well. Reputable exercise equipment manufacturers produce home versions such as treadmills and elliptical trainers that rival the quality of their more costly professional grade models.

One attraction of aerobic machines is their ease of use. Most pieces are built to accommodate a wide variety of fitness levels. Computer displays are common and can be simple or quite elaborate. You would typically input your age and weight as well as the workout program and intensity level you would like. Additional information may include the number of calories expended, pace, distance covered (in miles or kilometers), and heart rate. If included, pulse monitors that slip onto the earlobe or fingertip tend not to be as accurate as a chest strap transmitter. You would be advised to check their accuracy against your own manual pulse before relying upon these during your workouts.

If calories expended are provided realize that unless you are asked to supply your own body weight for the calculation, the expenditure is based on a 'typical user' such as a 150-pound male. Consider the information simply as a rough approximation if you are not asked to supply your body weight.

If your budget allows when purchasing home equipment, consider exercise equipment that would complement your established aerobic exercise mode by addressing an aspect of fitness that may be missing. For instance, a runner might outfit his home with a stationary bike. This choice would allow him to cross-train in different impact categories: running is high impact and weight-bearing whereas biking is non-weight-bearing. This would also offer an alternative when weather doesn't permit training outdoors.

When shopping for exercise equipment, always dress to move. Actually get on the equipment for a mini workout that lasts long enough to experience the features of the piece. Knowledgeable salespeople, DVD's accompanying your purchase, and manufacturers' websites can offer tips on how to get the most out of your equipment.

Intensity: How Hard Do I Need To Train?

In order to improve cardiorespiratory endurance, a substantial overload is necessary. During exercise, the heart rate usually increases linearly with the energy requirement. In other words, as the exercise gets increasingly more difficult your heart rate rises in a similarly increasing pattern. For this reason, the exercise heart rate has been used as a simple measure for estimating exercise intensity. Heart rate can be used to help you determine if you are exercising too hard or not hard enough to reach your fitness goals. Since there needs to

A WAY OF LIFE

Your exercise heart rate can be your coach, letting you know when to push harder and when to back off your efforts.

be an increase in exercise heart rate in order to achieve cardiorespiratory overload and subsequent improvement in endurance, the question is: How high should your heart rate be during aerobic exercise? Many years ago a study of young men yielded a minimum figure necessary for that increase. M. J. Karvonen, a Finnish researcher, found that to make appreciable gains in cardiorespiratory endurance, the heart rate during exercise must be raised by approximately 60 percent of the difference between the **resting** and **maximal heart rates**. More recent research has led the American College of Sports Medicine to expand its guidelines for a **target heart rate range**. A safe and reasonable intensity for most participants spans between 50 and 85 percent of the difference between resting and maximal heart rates. Calculating your target heart rate range is simple. First,

RESTING HEART RATE:
The lowest heart rate of the day, frequently determined first thing upon waking.

MAXIMAL HEART RATE:
The highest heart rate that a person's heart can achieve. It is usually determined during a maximal exercise test or can be predicted by subtracting your age from 220.

TARGET HEART RATE RANGE:
The intensity necessary to achieve cardiorespiratory overload and subsequent improvement in cardiorespiratory endurance; 50 to 85 percent of heart rate reserve, according to the American College of Sports Medicine.

find the difference between the maximal and resting rates. This is called the **heart rate reserve (HR reserve)**. Second, find the lower end of your range by multiplying that difference by

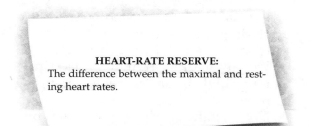

HEART-RATE RESERVE:
The difference between the maximal and resting heart rates.

.5. To find the upper end of your range, multiply that difference by .85. Add each result to the resting rate. This is called the **50 to 85 percent HR reserve**. In cases of overweight, musculoskeletal limitations, or after extended periods of inactivity you may want to start out at 40 to 60 percent HR reserve.

An illustration using a 40-year old man will make this calculation clear. His maximal heart rate can best be determined by a **maximal graded exercise test**, usually performed on a treadmill or bicycle ergometer. In a maximal test the workload is progressively increased and the heart rate steadily increases along with

MAXIMAL GRADED EXERCISE TEST:
A physical fitness/health assessment usually performed on a treadmill or bicycle ergometer. In a maximal test the workload is progressively increased and the heart rate steadily increases along with the workload until a point is reached at which the person can no longer continue the test. The heart rate at the point of maximal effort is considered the maximal heart rate.

$$(Max\ HR - Resting\ HR) \times .5 + Resting$$
HR = lower end of heart rate range
$$(Max\ HR - Resting\ HR) \times .85 + Resting$$
HR = upper end of heart rate range

the workload until a point is reached at which the man can no longer continue the test. His heart rate at the point of maximal effort is considered his maximal heart rate. If a maximal graded exercise test is not available, his maximal heart rate will have to be approximated by subtracting his age from 220. (Although reasonably accurate, this predicted maximal heart rate can be off 10-12 beats in either direction. Keep this in mind if, in practice, your target heart rate range seems slightly high or low.) This 40-year old's approximate maximal heart rate would be 220 - 40 = 180 beats per minute. His resting heart rate, determined first thing

The value of this substantial overload in eliciting a training effect has been well documented. In general, for most young adults this intensity means a target heart rate in the range of 150 to 170 beats per minute. For older adults, because of a typical decline in maximal heart rate with aging, a lower target heart rate may represent an adequate overload. A rate of 130 to 140 beats per minute may suffice. These intensities indicate safe and effective levels of vigorous exercise for healthy people.

How do you determine your heart rate during exercise?

To determine your exercise intensity you must find your pulse and count your heart rate during exercise, after you have broken a sweat and your breathing rate has increased or when you can describe your workout as 'moderately hard'. It is perfectly acceptable to stop for a brief moment to get a 10-second pulse count. Research studies reveal that this method gives a count indicative of your heart rate during exercise. Determining your heart rate relatively

A WAY OF LIFE

To approximate the highest heart rate you can achieve with all-out effort, your maximum heart rate, subtract your age from 220.

A WAY OF LIFE

If you don't have a pulse monitor, stop your activity for 10 seconds to get a count and multiply that number by 6 for your exercise heart rate.

upon waking may be 80 beats per minute. His HR reserve is the difference between his maximal and his resting (180 - 80), or 100 beats. Fifty percent of 100 is 50 beats. Adding this figure to his resting rate of 80, we get a target heart rate of 130 beats/minute, a safe and reasonable lower end of the range for that individual. To find the upper end of his range simply multiply HR reserve by 85 percent (100 x .85) and add that to his resting heart rate of 80. The highest heart rate in this 40-year old's target heart rate range, therefore, would be 165 beats/minute. The target heart rate range represents intensities that are safe and, most important, effective in producing a training effect on the cardiovascular system. Use this simple formula for arriving at your target heart rate range:

early into your workout either allows you to feel confident you are in your target heart rate range or signals you to adjust your intensity level either up or down. You will need a timing device such as a stopwatch, a wall clock, or a wristwatch with a second hand or digital readout.

Except in rare cases, the number of pulse beats your feel each minute is equal to your heart rate in beats per minute. Therefore, your heart rate can be counted at any convenient pulse point. Generally over the carotid artery in the neck, or on the inside of the wrist (radial artery) are the best places for feeling your pulse.

Taking your pulse on the inside of your wrist at the radial artery may be your best site. To do so, place the tips of two fingers (not the thumb) between the tendons and the wrist bone on the thumb side just below the wrist. Another site, the large artery in your neck can be located just under the jawbone and slightly in front of the prominent muscle on the side of your neck. Be sure to press lightly on your neck with fingers from that same side (don't cross over to the opposite side of the neck). A third site is on your chest, below and to the outside of your left nipple. When you stop momentarily for a pulse check it is important to locate it quickly to accurately reflect your pulse during movement. It will take a little practice, however, before you can consistently obtain a reliable pulse. In fact, you should first learn to count your resting pulse. Because your heart beats much slower at rest, counting the beats for 30 seconds and then multiplying by 2 is recommended. During exercise, the heart rate declines rapidly if you stop moving, so it is important for you to learn to count your pulse as soon as possible (within a second or two after stopping).

When you feel your pulse, count the beats for 10 seconds beginning with '1'. Then multiply your 10-second pulse count by 6 to determine your exercise heart rate in beats per minute. For example, a 10-second pulse count of 25 would indicate an exercise heart rate of 150 (25 x 6). If you wish to remember only your 10-second count as a short-hand for your full heart rate, that is fine.

If you find it difficult to accurately count your pulse, if you are exercising without a timing device, or if you are on a medication that affects your heart rate, you may also use the **rating of perceived exertion (RPE)** to monitor your intensity level. By verbally describing how the exercise effort feels, you train yourself to get in touch with how hard you are working. For example, in order to reap cardiorespiratory endurance benefits, your exercise effort should rate as 'moderately hard' to 'hard'. Research shows that RPE's closely relate to actual exercise heart rate and can be relied upon to guide workout intensity. We recommend you become adept at locating your pulse to determine exercise heart rate. Then learn to associate your target heart rate with an overall feeling of adequate exertion. Down the road, you may find you don't even need to check your pulse as often.

> **RATING OF PERCEIVED EXERTION (RPE):**
> A verbal description of how the exercise effort feels. RPE closely relates to actual exercise heart rate and can be relied upon to guide workout intensity.

What is speedplay?

Once you feel at home with your target heart rate range you can also incorporate '**speedplay**' into your aerobic workouts. Speedplay allows you to improve your level of cardiorespiratory endurance by introducing a more vigorous segment into your workout.

> **SPEEDPLAY:**
> A method for improving your level of cardiorespiratory endurance by introducing a more vigorous segment into your workout and interspersing brief recovery intervals of decreased intensity between your more vigorous work segments.

This more vigorous work segment is usually at the very upper end of your target heart rate range or even higher, approaching your maximal heart rate. Speedplay entails interspersing brief (30- to 60-second) recovery intervals of decreased intensity between your more vigor-

A WAY OF LIFE

In order to get faster at your particular aerobic activity, incorporate speedplay into your workouts for a relatively unstructured training tool.

ous work segments. For instance, if you are trying to speed up your swimming pace, push yourself as long as you can before you 'run out of breath' for the work interval. When you need a recovery interval, slow down for a short amount of time to return to your target heart rate range. These recovery intervals of milder exertion can occur whenever your body tells you to take a break. Don't stop moving altogether. Continuing to move at a lesser intensity allows the metabolic waste products (such as lactic acid) in your bloodstream to be eliminated faster than they would be during complete rest. Continued contraction of your large muscles also guarantees that your blood will continue to circulate back to your heart from your extremities. Speedplay, with its intermittent work/recovery periods, also allows you to extend a highly vigorous workout over a longer period of time. Furthermore, it ensures that your heart will pump rhythmically at a magnitude well above the resting rate throughout the complete workout. The conditioning that speedplay offers will better prepare you for your favorite sport, especially if you are competing in intense sports such as flag football, intramural basketball , soccer or tennis.

If you have been inactive, you may want to delay pursuing highly vigorous workouts like speedplay or sprint-type fitness activities which require sudden bursts of energy and quick movements until after you have built a solid fitness base. These types of activities are referred to as 'anaerobic' (without oxygen) and generally are high impact as well as high intensity. First establish a good level of cardiorespiratory fitness, muscular strength and endurance, and flexibility in order to reduce the chance of injury or excessive soreness. The older you grow, the more risky these activities become unless you are participating regularly in a physical fitness program. Inclu-

A WAY OF LIFE

Sprint-type, high intensity fitness activities which require sudden bursts of energy and quick movements are referred to as 'anaerobic' (without oxygen).

sion of these activities are usually necessary when preparing to compete in a particular sport.

Duration: How Long Do I Need To Train?

The duration of exercise is directly related to the intensity of the activity, your present fitness level, and your fitness goals. Exercise guidelines for healthy adults ages 18 to 65 years specify at least 30 minutes of moderate intensity aerobic exercise. However, if you train at vigorous intensities closer to 85% of your target heart rate range, the duration can drop to 20 minutes.

A WAY OF LIFE

The length of your cardiorespiratory workouts will depend on your exercise frequency, exercise intensity, your fitness level, and your goals.

For some beginners it may be unwise to immediately attempt a non-stop activity for 30 minutes. In this case, to avoid musculoskeletal injuries, to allow the cardiorespiratory system to adjust to new demands, and to prepare psychologically, begin with 20-minute sessions. Then proceed to increase your duration following the 'ten-percent rule'. This clear-cut rule of thumb dictates a ten percent increase in duration of your workouts from those of the previous week. It takes the guesswork out of determining how to safely increase your weekly workout duration. For instance, if your first week program starts successfully with 20-minute sessions, increase your duration by 2 minutes per session the following week. This may not sound like much of an increase.

TEN-PERCENT RULE:
An easy and safe guideline to follow concerning weekly increases in duration or distance of cardiorespiratory endurance training.

However, this ten percent weekly increase gradually accumulates added minutes so that before long you have achieved 30 minutes or more and have avoided the musculoskeletal injuries that often plague overambitious novice exercisers.

If you do not have a 30-minute block of time in which to exercise, you may break up your workout into three 10-minute sessions scattered throughout the day. Each 10-minute segment is like a 'mini-workout' and should be approached with the same attention to good form and intensity as a longer session. You still need to reach your target heart rate range, so your warm up and cool down don't count in the 10-minute total. The choice of activity can be the same each segment, or each can consist of a different aerobic mode.

Frequency: How Often Do I Need To Work Out?

Regular adherence to a moderately challenging program is necessary if you are to reach and maintain an adequate level of cardiorespiratory endurance. 'Weekend Warriors' who become vigorously active only on Saturday and Sunday, remaining sedentary throughout the rest of the week typically accomplish little more than sore muscles upon waking on Monday! The number of workouts per week, or frequency, needed to reach a cardiorespiratory training effect as established by the American College of Sports Medicine is 5 days for moderate intensity aerobic sessions. Vigorous sessions should take place at least 3 days per week. Physiological changes may occur as early as your first workout, with improvements in physical fitness building over a period of weeks. The first

few weeks will be a break-in period where perhaps 3 sessions allow you to feel successful and whet your appetite for more.

Your fitness workouts should be a regular part of your life. It's difficult to reach your fitness goals and remain motivated when your workouts are sporadic and occur only when convenient. Adherence to your fitness lifestyle day in and day out is of paramount importance! While daily workouts are not necessary to improve one's cardiorespiratory endurance, the routine they provide becomes almost an unconscious act, just like brushing your teeth. Daily workouts eliminate the tendency to dread the workout days and relish the 'off' days. Daily exercisers describe almost an addictively energetic feeling as a result of regular exercise and they truly miss that feeling when they absolutely don't have a chance to work out.

HOW DO I ADJUST YOUR EXERCISE PROGRAM IF I WANT TO LOSE WEIGHT?

Exercising to reduce body fat requires a different duration and frequency than those aimed at simply improving cardiorespiratory endurance. Losing one pound of body fat requires a person to expend 3,500 calories more than he or she takes in. In order to expend a significant amount of calories, performing cardiorespiratory endurance activities 5 to 7 days weekly for a duration of 45 minutes or more (closer to 60 to 90 minutes) are suggested. Progressing to this schedule using the 10 percent rule helps keep musculoskeletal injuries at bay.

A controversy exists over the best time of day to exercise in order to reduce body fat. Some research indicates that morning workouts use optimal amounts of fat for energy. Since the evidence is not conclusive at this point, it is wise to choose a time of day based on what fits your lifestyle. Plan to workout when you are feeling freshest, when you are least likely to make excuses to skip exercise, and at a time of day that provides your preferred climate. The morning workout, especially after one graduates and joins the workforce, may be the most convenient plan to stay regular with your exercise sessions. Some people exercise in the evening before dinner because exercise suppresses their appetite to some extent. Still others get too 'keyed up' with nighttime exercise and find it difficult to fall asleep. If possible, remain flexible concerning your workout time so that if unusual circumstances arise you can still fit your exercise session into your day.

WHAT ARE THE STEPS I SHOULD GO THROUGH TO PUT TOGETHER MY CARDIORESPIRATORY EXERCISE PROGRAM?

Designing your cardiorespiratory endurance exercise program is simple if you keep certain training specifics in mind.

1) Choose your MODE. Decide if you want to begin with only one activity or if you will be cross-training from the start. Purchase any needed equipment.

2) Start with a DURATION from 15 to 20 minutes, if possible. If you can not sustain nonstop activity for that duration, take rest breaks as needed. Be patient as you work progressively toward the 20-minute training goal. Continue to increase your duration to 30 minutes or longer using the ten-percent rule. If an additional goal is to reduce body fat, gradually work towards 45 minutes or longer (ideally 60 to 90 minutes).

3) Keep your heart rate in your target range of 50 to 85 percent HR reserve to achieve an adequate INTENSITY. Determine your training heart rate at least once during the middle of the conditioning portion of your workout to make sure you are in your target heart rate range.

4) Perform your activity/activities at a FREQUENCY of 3 to 5 days per week if your goal is solely cardiorespiratory endurance. If an additional goal is to reduce body fat, consider gradually working towards 5 to 7 days per week.

Finally, it is important to keep records of your aerobic workouts and we have provided training logs in Appendix B for your convenience. Training logs can be very detailed (see Figure 6.1) or relatively simple (see Figure 6.2). Keeping training logs not only helps you remember details of previous training sessions but can be very motivating by showing how far you have progressed. A more detailed discussion of keeping training records is covered in Chapter 10.

The following tips will help you decide which aerobic activities are available to you and will also give you some commonsense guidance if you have already chosen an activity. There is not enough space in these pages to go into deep detail on any one choice. We encourage you to become your own expert by reading books and magazines devoted to your activity. It would be wise to use the Web to gain the latest information on your aerobic exercise choice since research and technological improvements in equipment tend to change rapidly. Web sites and retail shops catering to your activity can put you in touch with other people in your area with the same interests who can continue to educate you via training groups.

What Are Some Tips To Help My Walking Program?

- Walking provides an adequate training stimulus as long as you maintain your target heart rate range by walking at a quick pace or up an incline.
- If you are trying to expend as much energy as possible in a given time period, running would be a better choice than walking. A brisk one-hour walk burns about 300 calories, whereas it takes only 30 minutes of running to burn about the same amount.
- Because walking is low-impact and running is high-impact, walking is usually less stressful on joints than running.

DATE	BODY WEIGHT	START TIME	EXERCISE MODE (Check all that apply)					DURATION / MILEAGE	HEART RATE (MIDWAY)
			Walk	Run	Bike	Swim	Row		
			Other:						

OTHER PERTINENT INFORMATION:

How did you feel before your workout?	Great	Good	Okay	Poor	Sick	Other:	
How did you feel during your workout?	Great	Good	Okay	Poor	Sick	Other:	
How did you feel after your workout?	Great	Good	Okay	Poor	Sick	Other:	
OVERALL WORKOUT SCORE	1 Worst	2	3	4	5 Best	Comments:	

What was the weather like? (Check all answers that apply)	Hot	Mild	Cold	Humid	Sunny	Cloudy	Other:
Was weather a factor in how you felt?	Yes	No	Comment:				

Have you been eating well?	Yes	No	Comment:
Was the 24 hours prior to your workout a <30% fat intake day?	Yes	No	If no, what foods put you over?
Are you staying well hydrated? (i.e. drinking 8-10 eight oz. glasses per day)	Yes	No	Comment

Are you feeling fatigued during the day?	Yes	No	Comment:
Are you sleeping well?	Yes	No	Comment:
Are you under unusual stress?	Yes	No	Comment:
Is your resting heart rate in the morning >10 bpm higher than normal?	Yes	No	If yes, closely look at your previous training logs and make adjustments in your workout, diet, and/or other habits to prevent overtraining.

Figure 6.1: Aerobic Exercise Log (Long Form)

- Walking for cardiorespiratory endurance is more than just strolling with the dog. Even though you've been walking most of your life, fitness walking requires paying attention to form and intensity.
- Let your heel land first and then roll onto the ball of your foot. Push off with your toes.
- As you become comfortable, begin to pick up your pace. If it feels natural to lengthen your stride, extend your leg and foot farther in front and push off farther behind. Once you find a stride length that suits you, do not attempt to continuously lengthen the stride in order to increase your speed. Instead, rely on taking more steps per minute and pumping your arms more vigorously.
- Maintaining a right angle bend at your elbow, let your arms swing parallel to the body in a relaxed and rhythmic manner in opposition to your feet. Your

DATE	BODY WEIGHT	START TIME	EXERCISE MODE	DURATION / MILEAGE	HEART RATE (MIDWAY)

COMMENTS:

DATE	BODY WEIGHT	START TIME	EXERCISE MODE	DURATION / MILEAGE	HEART RATE (MIDWAY)

COMMENTS:

DATE	BODY WEIGHT	START TIME	EXERCISE MODE	DURATION / MILEAGE	HEART RATE (MIDWAY)

COMMENTS:

DATE	BODY WEIGHT	START TIME	EXERCISE MODE	DURATION / MILEAGE	HEART RATE (MIDWAY)

COMMENTS:

Figure 6.2: Aerobic Exercise Log (Simplified Form)

hands can reach the level of your shoulders in front and your hip joint in back.
- Avoid swinging your arms across the front of your body, as this slows you down and may cause your torso to twist, increasing the chance of strain to joints down the chain.
- For some people, using a treadmill beats exercising outside in the dark or in inclement weather. The intensity of a workout can be readily controlled by adjusting the speed or the incline of the treadmill.
- Treadmills are handy for walkers and runners living in flat areas who desire to train on hilly terrain by creating hills through manipulating the height and duration exercised on an incline. Setting the treadmill at an incline is one way to elevate the heart rate into the

target range. It also allows increased use of the 'climbing muscles', the quadriceps on the front of the thighs and the gluteals (buttocks). For additional motivation, a programmable treadmill varies the speed and incline automatically over a pre-selected period of time, working within specific intensities of your target heart rate range.

What Are Some Tips To Help My Running Program?

- Minute for minute, running is one of the most effective cardiorespiratory and energy-expending activities.
- High quality running and walking shoes last from 300 to 500 miles. Remember your purchase date by writing it in indelible ink somewhere on the shoe. Check a calendar and extrapolate your expected 300-mile date based on your current weekly mileage. Write that date on the shoe as well to remind you when it's time to consider new shoes.
- The run-walk technique of conditioning can be used all by itself as a highly effective aerobic activity or as a steppingstone for beginning a running program.
- Start a run-walk program by first running 110 to 220 yards (or 100 to 200 meters on a track) followed by 30-second periods of brisk walking. These run-walk combinations are repeated throughout the workout. The walking segments are an important part of this continuous rhythmic routine because they represent a recovery period. However, the heart rate must remain in the target range regardless of whether you walk or run.
- Don't run on your toes. Beginning runners who start this way quickly learn this is incorrect unless running a short distance sprint. A relative flat foot or the heel-to-the-ball of the foot techniques are the accepted ways of fitness running.

- Over-striding is a common fault of many inexperienced runners. Over-striding results in the lead foot striking the ground too far ahead of your body, causing a jerky inefficient style that is tough on the knee joint. There is an optimal stride length for you. Experiment to find one that allows you to cover a good distance with each step without asking your hip, knee and ankle joints to go beyond their comfortable range of motion.
- Run with relaxed hands. Clenching your fists can signal other muscle groups to tighten up, detracting from a fluid running form. If you sense yourself tightening your hands, periodically pretend to play a piano with your fingers to loosen up. Another trick is to carry the cardboard from an empty toilet paper roll in each hand. Get through your entire workout without crushing it.
- Other common faults include running with toes pointing inward or outward, excessive bouncing, carrying the arms and hands too high (above the shoulders), and swinging the hands across the center line of the body. Strive to run as smoothly as possible, eliminating all excess movements.
- To make sure you are working within your own capacity, try the 'talk test' while you're running. If you cannot carry on a conversation without becoming short of breath, then you're probably overexerting. If you can sing, however, you are not working hard enough!
- Running on a treadmill or on land is high impact in that at some point both feet are off the ground. Some treadmill manufacturers claim that their treadmill 'gives' by allowing slight flexing of the bed for improved shock absorption over road running. However, it is questionable whether this feature reduces the impact forces enough so that individuals experiencing overuse injuries can have a safe, comfortable workout. It may be more advisable to choose a low- or non-impact activity during recovery.

What Are Some Tips To Help My Biking Program?

- Cycling, an excellent non-weight-bearing alternative to running, can provide a good excuse to be outdoors, much needed for the majority of us who work or study indoors.

- During unforgiving weather one option for cyclists who prefer their outdoor bike to an indoor stationary cycle is to invest in a 'spin trainer'. Cyclists mount their outdoor bike on this type of bike stand which keeps the wheels from contacting the floor during temporary indoor use.

- If comfort is a concern, try a recumbent bicycle. Recumbents come in outdoor or indoor stationary models. Recumbent seats resemble chairs with wide seats and back supports. The foot pedals are located in front of you instead of underneath you, and frequently the handlebars are found under your hips or directly in front to eliminate shoulder fatigue. Tandem recumbent bikes provide an excellent workout for cyclists of different fitness levels, as each person provides power independently of the other.

- Naturally, the speed at which you ride will determine your cycling intensity. In general, riding at a pace of 4 to 5 minutes per mile (12 to 15 mph) is equivalent to a 50 to 85 percent HR reserve intensity for most people. Choose a bike that allows you to shift through a variety of gears that adapt as your fitness level advances as well as when terrain changes.

- Before embarking on a cycling training program, allow yourself adequate practice time to become familiar with the brakes, shifting into the different gears, and high-speed riding.

- Because you are considered a vehicle when on a bike, ride on the right-hand side of public roads. Also, use hand signals to indicate turns and stopping and obey traffic signals as if you were driving an automobile. If riding with other cyclists on busy roads where the posted speed is faster than that of the group's and passing is difficult, ride single file to avoid frustrating drivers.

- A qualified professional at a reputable cycling store will help you choose either a mountain bike (wider, deep-tread tires), a road/racing bike (narrower, smooth tires) or a hybrid of the first two, depending on where and how you intend to ride.

- Regardless of the type of bike you ride, a time clock and odometer should be standard equipment for checking heart rate and pace per mile. Like most cardiorespiratory equipment currently available, heart rate monitors may be built in or easily added to your bike.

- When you are sitting on a bike seat with the balls of your feet on the pedals, your knee joint should be slightly bent when the pedal is at its lowest point. This alignment places the large thigh muscles in an advantageous position when you pedal and should be comfortable on your knees. Strain at the knee joint is what you will feel if your seat is set too low Toe clips allow you to utilize not only the hip and knee extensor muscles as the pedal is pushed downward but engage the flexor muscles to help pull the pedal back up again.

- If cycling in the dark is your only opportunity, make certain you are as visible to drivers as possible from the greatest distance. Mount both bright front lights and rear strobe lights on your bike, and wear obvious reflective material on a vest, your cycling shorts, and shoes.

- You reduce your risk of head injury by 85 percent and brain injury by almost 90 percent when you wear a helmet. The Bicycle Federation of America states that the consumer can be confident in the safety and durability of a helmet as long as it bears one of the safety stickers indicating that the helmet has been certified by the American National Standards Institute (ANSI) or the Snell Memorial Foundation.

- If country roads are easily accessible they tend to provide more non-stop workouts than do city streets. In fact, if they are within a 10-minute ride, many cyclists use the slower city street riding as their warm up. By the time they reach the less-traveled roads, their heart rates have just reached their target ranges.

- For cross training, consider alternating a day of running outside with a day of indoor cycling on a stationary bike. Another idea is to combine the stationary bike with one or more machines in a single workout session to balance your fitness program.

- Less expensive stationary bikes rely on resistance (how hard it is to pedal) from a flywheel with a belt on it or a fan wheel that generates air resistance. The faster you ride, the more difficult the workload. These bikes are usually equipped with ergometers that measure the work performed. Some bikes are dual action: the handlebars can be pumped back and forth to exercise the arms, chest, and back while pedaling. Just make sure you actually pull and push instead of just resting your hands on this type of handlebar. Electronic bikes allow you to choose both your resistance and pedal frequency. The workload is generally measured in watts. With computerized displays these bikes can be more costly.

What Are Some Tips To Help My Swimming Program?

- Swimming is a superb cardiorespiratory endurance exercise choice for people who are unable to participate in weight-bearing activities. The involvement of the upper body muscles in particular makes swimming an excellent cross training choice. Couple swimming with other aerobic exercise forms like walking, running, or cycling for total body involvement.

- Because swimming offers four basic strokes to choose from (freestyle/front crawl, backstroke, breast stroke, and butterfly), combining two or more strokes within a workout can minimize the chance of suffering overuse injuries. A simple variation of strokes offers an abbreviated rest for one muscle group while allowing other muscle groups to be actively exercised and stimulated.

- Home pools that are too short to provide good lap swimming can become very useful when set up for tethered swimming. A simple piece of rubberized tubing with one end attached around a swimmer's ankle or waist and the other end around any immovable object on the perimeter of the pool (such as a ladder or diving board stand) can provide just enough stretch and resistance to swim in place. This tubing can also be tossed into a suitcase and used at a hotel pool when on business trips or vacations.

- Increase the drag of the water and thus the workout intensity by wearing multiple swimsuits or even a mesh swim vest with pockets that catch the water as you move forward in the pool. Just make sure you don't alter your stroke in the process.

- Swimming is the one aerobic activity that differs in your normal target heart rate range. It is well documented that when you are prone (lying face down in the water) your heart rate is anywhere from 8 to 12 beats lower than when you exercise upright. Keep this in mind and don't get frustrated if you fall short of your usual land-based target range. Determine your special swimming target range or rely on perceived exertion, swimming at an intensity of 'moderately hard' to 'hard'.

- Keeping track of your exercise heart rate in the pool can be as simple as checking your pulse using a pace clock, usually found on a pool deck or wall. Alternately, waterproof heart rate monitors similar to those worn on land are available for swimmers.
- Swimmers often choose hand paddles, kick boards, and swim fins to sharpen their 'feel' of the water and to make body position adjustments in the water. It is important not to warm up with these aids, as they over-exaggerate limb movements and may irritate the joints. It is also not a good idea to use them as a crutch for poor technique.
- Freestyle (front crawl) is the fastest stroke and would therefore be the stroke of choice when you are trying to maximize your workout distance in a given time. Butterfly requires both arms to leave the water at once and therefore is the most strenuous of the four strokes. Swimming a few lengths of 'fly' would certainly elevate a sluggish heart rate into the target range (and maybe beyond!).
- To vary your workout swim a different stroke every four lengths. Changing strokes systematically (such as four lengths freestyle, four lengths backstroke, and four lengths breaststroke) also eases the task of counting lengths completed.
- If you are an unskilled swimmer your workout can be productive if you are able to swim at least one length of the pool (usually 25 yards or meters). A simple workout is to swim one length of the pool, then climb out and walk back to the other end of the pool where you started. Repeat this procedure for the workout duration. In some situations it may not be possible to get out of the pool to walk. Instead, you may choose to rest in the water at the end of the pool. Moderate movements of the legs as you rest will aid your recovery between vigorous swims. Alternately, if

the pool is shallow enough, your walking can take place in the water where you have the added benefit of its resistance to keep your heart rate in the target range. This swim-walk routine is similar to the walk-run technique we have already described.

What Are Some Tips To Help My Aerobics/Aerobic Dance Program?

- Since the 1970's, aerobic dance or 'aerobics' has been a motivating form of cardiorespiratory endurance exercise for those who love music. Remember, the term "aerobic" literally means 'with oxygen'. Aerobics can take the form of choreographed aerobic dance, high-impact, low-impact, or high/low-impact aerobics. Classes may combine two or more of these forms within the same workout.
- Choreographed aerobic dance consists of routines that typically repeat movements when phrases in the music repeat. The routines remain the same from workout to workout which builds confidence and freedom to enjoy moving without requiring too much concentration. One drawback is the necessity to stop and learn each routine at its introduction. The target heart rate range is difficult to maintain in this instance.
- Aerobics shoes differ from running shoes by providing more shock-absorption at the ball and arch of the foot where landing takes place. There are also no 'waffles' or nubs on the soles that could interfere with the typical twisting and lateral sliding movements.
- Just as important as the type of shoe you wear is the surface on which you perform aerobics. Never exercise on concrete or linoleum and stay away from carpet if possible (it is easy to catch your foot on the carpet nap). Request wooden flooring, particularly floors suspended over air space or additional shock-absorbent materials.

What Are Some Tips To Help My Water Aerobics/Water Running Program?

- Aerobics performed in a swimming pool offers an additional exercise choice for people who are prone to musculoskeletal injuries. These individuals benefit from the buoyancy of the water which reduces joint stresses associated with weight-bearing exercise. This makes water aerobics a natural choice for overweight/obese exercisers or those with arthritis.
- Because water offers 12 times the resistance of air, muscles must work much harder to maintain tempo while performing the same movements they would on land.
- Make sure a water aerobics instructor's goals are the same as yours. Many classes claim to be 'water aerobics' but do very little to condition the cardiovascular system. Instead, these classes spend time isolating particular muscle groups and performing exercises meant to increase muscular strength and endurance. While developing muscular strength and endurance is always encouraged, the heart rates achieved with these exercises do not reach and/or maintain the 50 to 85 percent HR reserve level. Focus instead on continuous, rhythmic, large muscle movements.
- Additional equipment can be used to increase intensity by increasing drag. These include wearing baggy shirts and shorts, webbed hand gloves, or hand-held fans and buoys to pull and push against the water.
- Water running may not be familiar to many but can provide a highly vigorous cardiorespiratory conditioning workout. Developed for highly-trained but injured runners seeking an alternative activity that would help maintain their cardiorespiratory fitness as they healed, water running has become a well-kept secret for recreational exercisers as well. It entails wearing a buoyant belt or 'aqua jogger' that allows you to keep your body submerged in deep water while your head clears the water. By vigorously moving your legs in a running motion and quickly pumping your arms you soon experience the resistance that water provides.
- Water running may be performed freely as you move around in a pool's deep end or in a lake. You also can tether the back of the belt to a pool ladder or diving board stand or dock with a long piece of rubberized tubing that keeps you in one place. Water running is most fun when performed with another person or with waterside music.

What Are Some Tips To Help My Step Aerobics Program?

- Often called bench aerobics, step aerobics originated as a low-impact activity since one foot was always in contact with either the step or the floor. It quickly evolved into a high-impact activity that included jumps and hops. A knowledgeable instructor handles both types by first demonstrating a low impact step followed by its high impact version so that you can choose.
- Movements facing the step mainly use muscles from the front and back of the hip and thigh. Straddling the step involves the outer and inner thigh muscles to a much higher degree. Calf and shin muscle groups are recruited every time you step up and down. Upper body involvement can be as much or as little as needed to reach your target heart rate range.
- Step aerobics can help condition the muscle groups surrounding the knee and hip joints. Correct step height creates a bend in the knee no deeper than a right angle when the foot is flat on the bench. Each base added to a step typically raises the height 2 inches. Experiment with these bases to find the correct step height for your stature and cardiorespiratory endurance level.

What Are Some Tips To Help My Rope Jumping Program?

- For exercisers who travel, tossing a jump rope into their suitcase provides an accessible activity while on the road.
- Choose a good rope long enough to reach from armpit to armpit while passing under both feet. The models with plastic disks that slide around the rope provide a good balance and weight to the rope. Also, handles that are slightly weighted will help keep the rope from getting tangled.
- Keep your arms relaxed close to your side and allow your wrists to do the turning of the rope.
- Beginners can skip (step-hop) with each revolution while more advanced jumpers hop only once per revolution. As you move from beginner to advanced category, increase workout intensity either by increasing speed from 80 revolutions per minute to more than 120 or by using a weighted rope. A metronome or music with the right tempo can help you establish your speed.

What Are Some Tips To Help My In-Line Skating Program?

- In-line skating is low-impact and involves the large muscle groups of the hips and thighs. The more proficient skaters lean their trunks forward, almost parallel to the ground. This requires very strong trunk muscles (as beginners trying to emulate this posture quickly learn).
- Intensity of exercise with in-line skating can be modified by adjusting speed and the amount of muscles used to propel and balance. Hills, of course, also offer increased work on the way up for a skater. However, downhill skating requires much less energy and much more control and skill. Even beginner skaters can increase energy expenditure by making leg movements forceful and wide-ranging. Arms swinging purpose-fully in opposition or held in typical racing position with one behind the back can also improve form and increase speed.
- In-line skating can be combined with other outdoor aerobic activities for unique cross training. Heading out for a 20-minute run that loops back to your skates, quickly changing equipment and then heading out for a 20-minute skate then looping back to your bike for a final 20-minute ride offers a high-impact/low-impact/non-impact combination workout.

ARE THERE OTHER TYPES OF CARDIORESPIRATORY ENDURANCE EXERCISE EQUIPMENT & ACTIVITIES?

- Elliptical machines are highly popular in part because the motions involved are very natural. Instead of simply sliding your legs forward and backward like cross-country skiing or in the circular motion of a bicycle, the legs move in a more natural ellipse. A large range of motion at the hips, knees, and ankles is possible.
- Elliptical machines with arm poles allow more upper body muscle involvement than those where you rest your arms on railings. Adding arm motions can increase your heart rate and energy expenditure.
- Involving the upper body is not the only way to increase intensity on an elliptical machine. Move your legs (and arms) more quickly to speed up your pace. If the machine allows, increase the resistance of both the legs and arms.
- Rowing is an excellent non-weight-bearing aerobic activity. A good workout is experienced without high-impact stress to your lower body. It also requires involvement of the lower back, abdominal, arm, and shoulder muscles.
- Machine rowing should simulate the actual work of rowing a boat. The push of your legs moves the seat back and

forward on a metal frame while arms pull a handlebar attached to a chain or cable pulley. To begin the rowing movement, legs extend softly at hips and knees (take care not to hyperextend) followed by arms completing a pull as shoulder blades squeeze together. The recovery begins as the arms extend with control towards the flywheel, followed by flexing the knees and hips as the seat returns forward. The speed and the force with which you pull determines the resistance that you work against. It is important that the trunk remains mostly erect throughout.

- The stair-climber is most effective when the exerciser moves the legs through their full range of motion rather than small, quick pulsing presses. Maintain good upright posture, and try to avoid leaning your body weight on the frame when you become fatigued. Most machines can be programmed for various effort levels, such as offering a feature that allows you to exercise at a rate of 4 to 17 times your resting energy level. You must keep your legs moving continuously on a stair-climber or the steps will 'bottom out'.

- Can you guess which elite athletes have the greatest aerobic capacity values ever recorded? Cross-country skiers! Cross-country skiing offers the best potential for cardiorespiratory conditioning because it involves every major muscle group and requires plenty of energy. During this non-impact activity, arms, shoulders, chest and back muscles must pull and reach. Legs and hips must flex and extend in a wide range of motion. Trunk muscles must maintain erect posture and help a skier stay in balance.

- Indoor ski machines offer exercisers who never have access to snow a chance to master outdoor skiing techniques while receiving excellent aerobic exercise. One exception is the technique of 'skating'. This is not possible on a cross-country ski machine due to the machine's parallel tracks that restrict movement to a straight path.

SUMMARY

This chapter provided information that will help you begin a cardiorespiratory endurance program that is geared to your capabilities while adequately stimulating your heart, lungs, and muscles. Developing your own personal aerobic exercise program is easy if you follow the guidelines discussed. Regardless of the activity you choose, it is important to sustain a target heart rate well above resting but not at an exhaustive level. As you progress in your conditioning, you will be able to do more exercise at the same target heart rate, accomplishing more work with the same sensation of effort. So if your heart rate is 162 while running a 10-minute-mile pace at the start of a program, after three months of training you may be able to run an 8:30-mile pace at the same heart rate. You will perform more work in the same amount of time, increasing your cardiorespiratory endurance and burning more calories per minute. Remember, you can always improve and set new goals with a variety of activities throughout your life. Be open to the myriad of possibilities!

7 Improving Muscular Strength and Endurance

A muscle must be subjected to greater-than-normal loads to be strengthened. For most people, daily activities do not adequately stimulate their muscles enough to cause strength and endurance increases. Even individuals who lead active lifestyles rarely participate in activities strenuous enough to elicit strength gains. Therefore, with advancing age, people typically lose strength. In fact, the loss of strength with age is so common that it has been thought to be a direct result of the aging process. However, research now indicates that

> ### A WAY OF LIFE
>
> For most people, daily activities do not adequately stimulate the muscles enough to maintain muscular strength and endurance as we age.

the majority of strength loss associated with aging is due to the lack of activity intense enough to maintain strength. Thus, as we grow older, we need to perform specific exercises of sufficient intensity on a regular basis to effectively develop and/or maintain muscular strength and endurance. These exercises are collectively known as **resistance exercises**.

> ### A WAY OF LIFE
>
> Resistance exercises of sufficient intensity need to be performed on a regular basis to effectively develop and/or maintain muscular strength and endurance.

They force the muscles being worked to generate more tension by providing an additional resistance against which the muscles must act. The most common form of resistance exercise is weight lifting, but exercises using body weight (e.g. calisthenics), elastic bands and partner-assisted exercises also fall under the category of resistance exercise.

> **RESISTANCE EXERCISES:**
> Any exercises that provide a load against which muscles must exert force. The most recognized form of resistance exercise is weight lifting. However exercises using body weight, stretching elastic bands, and pulling against a partner are also resistance exercises.

Read the following questions and formulate in your mind what you perceive to be the correct answer. If you don't know the answer, then read the chapter with the intent of finding the answer. If you did answer the question, then read the chapter to make sure your answer is correct and not a misconception regarding ways to improve muscular strength and endurance.

- What's the difference between muscular strength and muscular endurance?
- What are the benefits of resistance training?
- What are the training specifics (i.e. frequency, intensity, and duration) for designing a resistance training program?
- Are bodybuilding and strength training the same thing?

- What are some basic guidelines that should be followed when resistance training?
- Does resistance training require special clothing, training aids and/or equipment?
- What exercises would you choose for a resistance training program designed to work all the major muscles of the body?

WHAT IS THE DIFFERENCE BETWEEN MUSCULAR STRENGTH AND ENDURANCE?

Muscular strength, as mentioned in Chapter 1, is the ability of a muscle or group of muscles to generate maximal force. For example, the maximum amount of weight you can bench press one time represents the muscular

> **MUSCULAR STRENGTH:**
> The ability of a muscle or group of muscles to generate maximal force. For example, the maximum amount of weight you can bench press one time represents the muscular strength of your chest, arms, and shoulders.

strength of your chest, arms, and shoulders. **Muscular endurance** is the ability of a muscle or group of muscles to resist fatigue while either repeatedly generating or sustaining forceful muscle actions. Muscle strength and endurance are discussed together in this chapter because resistance training can improve both.

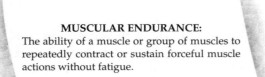

> **MUSCULAR ENDURANCE:**
> The ability of a muscle or group of muscles to repeatedly contract or sustain forceful muscle actions without fatigue.

How, you may ask, does resistance training improve both? Simply put, resistance train-

ing improves strength, which in turn, serves as the basis for muscular endurance. A stronger muscle is able to perform more **repetitions** with a fixed weight than a weaker muscle and therefore will demonstrate greater endurance.

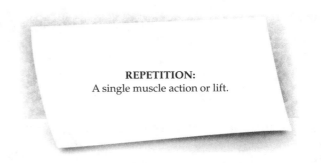

> **REPETITION:**
> A single muscle action or lift.

A good example of how strength can effect muscular endurance is using the one-minute pushup test. A person with strong chest, arm, and shoulder muscles will be able to do more pushups than a person who has weak muscles and thus will demonstrate greater muscle endurance. In this chapter, the training principles and guidelines for resistance training will be discussed so you can develop an effective program for improving both muscular strength and muscular endurance.

A WAY OF LIFE

Strong muscles are able to perform more repetitions with a fixed amount of weight than weak muscles and therefore will demonstrate greater muscular endurance.

WHAT ARE THE BENEFITS OF MUSCULAR STRENGTH AND ENDURANCE?

Muscular strength is perhaps the most underappreciated and neglected component of physical fitness. Strong muscles often are seen merely as an attribute needed by athletes for maximizing sport performance. However, strong muscles not only improve athletic performance but also make work and leisure activities less taxing and more enjoyable. Thus adequate levels of strength have a positive impact on the quality of life. Although most people recognize the importance of cardiorespiratory exercise and its impact on health, few know about muscle strength and its role as a health-related component of physical fitness (see Table 7.1).

Strong muscles help prevent injuries in athletic competition and during daily activities by lending structural integrity to the joints they cross. The joints of the body are surrounded by muscles or the **tendons** of muscles, which assist the **ligaments** in holding the articulating

TENDON:
A fibrous connective tissue that attaches muscle to bone.

bones together. The stronger the muscles, the greater their potential for resisting forces that could disrupt or injure the normal anatomy of the joint. In addition, strong muscles themselves are less prone to injury. The connective

LIGAMENT:
A fibrous connective tissue that holds two or more bones together.

tissues that hold the muscle together, as well as attach them to the bones, become thicker, stronger, and less prone to tearing. The connective tissue harness becomes stronger because the connective tissue cells, like muscle cells, are stimulated by resistance training. They pro-

duce more **collagen**, which is the fibrous material that gives connective tissue its strength. The end result is stronger connective tissues that are more resistant to tearing or ripping whenever the muscles generate force.

COLLAGEN:
A type of protein that forms connective tissues such as ligaments and tendons.

Resistance training also leads to improvements in other components of physical fitness, such as muscular endurance, muscular power, and body composition. As mentioned previously, muscular strength can improve **absolute muscular endurance**. For example, before strength training, you might be able to do eight

ABSOLUTE MUSCULAR ENDURANCE:
The ability of a muscle or group of muscles to resist fatigue when exerting force against an object with a constant weight.

bicep curls with 70 pounds before fatiguing, but after six weeks of strength training, you might be able to perform 20 repetitions with 70 pounds. In other words, your muscle endurance when lifting the same amount of weight (i.e. 70 pounds) has improved. In addition, strength training increases **muscular power**. Muscular power is also known as

MUSCULAR POWER:
The ability of a muscle or group of muscles to generate force at high movement speeds. Also known as "speed-strength".

speed-strength because it depends on both speed of movement and the ability of muscle to generate force. Resistance training improves muscular strength and, as a result, can directly impact muscular power.

Resistance training also improves body composition by increasing lean body weight (muscle, connective tissue, and bone) and decreasing fat weight. (To evaluate your body fat see Chapter 3.) Some people who are not overly fat may actually gain body weight despite losing body fat with a resistance training program simply because muscle weighs more than fat. However, be careful! Large increases in body weight may suggest you are consuming more calories than you are burning through exercise. Normally the increase in lean body mass due to resistance training will not exceed 7 to 12 pounds over the course of a year's training.

An additional benefit of increasing lean body mass through resistance training is that it increases the body's metabolism. Exercise scientists know that the body must expend more energy (calories) to maintain muscle tissue than it does to maintain fat tissue. The increased metabolic rate not only results in loss of body fat but also makes it easier for individuals to maintain or control a favorable body composition.

Muscles also serve as the body's shock absorbers. They dampen the impact forces that normally occur during walking, running, and other activities. Without good shock absorbers (that is, strong muscles) over time these impact forces can damage the **cartilage** in joints. This may ultimately result in degenerative diseases such as osteoarthritis. In addition, strong muscles can help prevent common ailments such as lower-back pain. It is well documented that one of the key contributing factors to lower-

CARTILAGE:
A very smooth type of connective tissue found in the joints between bones that helps to protect the bones and provides a smooth surface for movement.

back pain is poor muscular strength, specifically of abdominal and lower back muscles. Common remedies for back pain, such as heat application or medication, don't target the primary cause, which for many individuals are weak muscles. But if muscular weakness is the problem, resistance training offers a long-term solution rather than a short-term treatment.

Finally, resistance training is also an effective way of building strong, dense bones. This is particularly important for individuals who have been diagnosed or are at risk for **osteoporosis**, a disease resulting in porous, brittle bones. All too often, we think of bone tissue as "lifeless" because that is how it is presented. In

OSTEOPOROSIS:
A bone disease in which the quantity and density of bone becomes so low that the bones become brittle and easy to fracture

anatomy laboratories, the bony skeleton hangs in the corner, its bones white, dry, and lifeless looking. However, it is important to remember that in living, breathing individuals, the bones are made up of living cells, just like all the other tissues in the body. And as with muscle and connective tissue cells, bone cells respond to resistance training by making the bone tissue denser and thus better able to support loads and resist breaking.

Table 7.1. Benefits of Muscular Strength and Endurance Training

- Increases Muscular Strength
- Increases Muscular Endurance
- Increases Muscular Power
- Increases Muscle Mass
- Increases Bone Density
- Increases Connective Tissue Strength
- Decreases Risk for Injury
- Helps Maintain a Favorable Body Composition
- Improves Physical Appearance
- Improves Quality of Life

In this chapter, we will present guidelines for developing muscular strength and endurance. Keep in mind that the focus is not on developing large bulky muscles, as in bodybuilding, but on building stronger muscles. Combining strengthening exercises with your chosen cardiorespiratory activities will further improve your physical fitness and help you get the most out of life.

WHAT ARE SOME COMMONLY HELD RESISTANCE TRAINING MISCONCEPTIONS?

Although resistance training in various forms has been practiced for over 2,500 years, most of our current information is based on research performed since the 1960s. Despite the growing popularity of resistance training among men and women, however, there is still a lack of scientifically established training guidelines. Many of the training practices have stood the test of time in the sense that they must work or they would not still be around. Unfortunately many misconceptions have been perpetuated as well.

One misconception is that resistance training will make you muscle bound, inflexible, and slow. All of these would be disastrous to any athlete or physically active individual. In truth, a properly designed and executed resistance training program will do just the opposite. Not only can it increase flexibility, it can improve muscular strength and endurance, speed, and jumping ability. In fact, many of the world's fastest athletes use resistance training to enhance their sport performance. Not only that, Olympic weight lifters are second in flexibility only to gymnasts.

Another misconception is that **strength training** is the same as **bodybuilding**. Nothing could be further from the truth. *They are not the same.* Strength training is not going to make you the next Arnold Schwarzenegger.

> **BODYBUILDING:**
> A type of exercise program designed specifically to cause as much muscle enlargement as possible. Bodybuilding is also a sport in which the competitors are judged on muscle development and symmetry.

Although individuals involved in these activities perform resistance exercises, strength trainers and bodybuilders train to attain different goals. The goal of competitive bodybuilding is to put on as much muscle mass and to get as large as possible. In fact, one of the reasons why the muscle bound misconception still prevails is because most people incorrectly associate strength training with the large bodybuilders. Strength training is designed to make your muscles stronger, not necessarily larger. Bodybuilders spend many hours every day training to develop their muscles, whereas strength training may involve only 45 to 90 minutes of training two to three times per week. The amount of time most people spend strength training simply isn't adequate for the increases in muscle mass produced by a bodybuilding workout.

Along the same lines is the misguided suggestion that women should not strength train because of its masculinizing effects. Certainly strength training can cause some **muscle hypertrophy** but not to the degree it does in males. Additionally, it does not deepen women's voices and cause hair to grow on their chests. In other words, strength training does not cause increases in circulating levels of

> **STRENGTH TRAINING:**
> An exercise program that is designed specifically to increase muscular strength, not muscle size.

> **MUSCLE HYPERTROPHY:**
> The enlargement of muscle usually resulting from resistance training.

the male hormone testosterone. Remember, it is testosterone and not resistance training that controls masculinity.

WHAT ARE THE RESISTANCE TRAINING SPECIFICS?

The resistance training specifics vary depending on the goal of your exercise program. In the following sections, we will discuss the details of how to get what you want from your resistance training program.

What type of exercise should I perform?

Muscular strength and endurance are increased through resistance exercises. Resistance exercises challenge the musculoskeletal system by increasing the amount of force necessary to perform a particular movement or activity. Weight lifting using **free weights** is the most common form of resistance exercise.

> **FREE WEIGHTS:**
> Equipment such as bars, weight plates, dumbbells and barbells used in resistance training.

However, resistance exercises also can involve lifting other types of heavy objects, lifting body weight, pulling against elastic bands, and even pushing or pulling forcefully against immovable objects or training partners. Regardless of the type of resistance exercises used, as long as the load is intense enough to stress the musculoskeletal system, the muscles will become stronger and the bones will become denser.

Resistance exercises involve two basic types of muscular actions—static and dynamic. Training involving **static muscle actions** is known as **isometric training**. In isometric training, no limb movement occurs during performance of the exercise despite the fact that the muscle is generating maximal force. An example of an arm and shoulder isometric exercise would be standing in a doorway and pressing your hands against the doorframe.

> **STATIC MUSCLE ACTION:**
> Muscle activity that generates high force output but no joint movement.

> **ISOMETRIC TRAINING:**
> A mode of resistance training involving static muscle actions.

Because no joint or limb movement is involved, isometric training is often used in clinical settings for rehabilitation after injury or surgery. Although strength gains resulting from isometric training have been documented, most authorities agree that resistance exercises involving movement produce the best results. Thus, the information presented in this chapter pertains exclusively to resistance exercises involving **dynamic muscle actions**.

> **DYNAMIC MUSCLE ACTION:**
> Muscle activity that results in joint movement.

Dynamic exercises are resistance exercises that involve joint movement. The muscle actions causing the movement can be the result of either **concentric actions** or **eccentric actions**. The most common form of dynamic resistance exercise is known as **isotonic exercise**. It involves lifting a fixed amount of weight (i.e. dumbbell or barbell) a specific number of times. Because most daily activities and sports involve dynamic types of muscle actions rather than isometric contractions and because of the

CONCENTRIC ACTION:
A type of muscle action in which force is generated while the muscle shortens. Concentric muscle actions are performed during the up-phase of a lift.

REPETITIONS MAXIMUM (RM):
The maximum load that can be lifted a given number of times. For example, 6RM refers to the maximum weight that can be lifted six but not seven times.

ECCENTRIC ACTION:
A type of muscle action in which force is generated while the muscle lengthens. Eccentric muscle actions are performed during the lowering phase of a lift.

REPETITION:
A single muscle action or lift.

specificity principle of training (see Chapter 4), dynamic exercises are the most widely recommended.

ISOTONIC EXERCISE:
A dynamic mode of resistance training in which the muscles generate force against a constant resistance, such as when performing a bench press with an 80-pound barbell.

How heavy should the weight be?

The difficulty (i.e. intensity) of a resistance training exercise is determined by the load you are lifting or the resistance you are working against. The lighter the load the lower the intensity and the more repetitions you can perform. The term **repetition,** or "rep" for short, refers to the number of muscle contractions or lifts performed in succession without rest. For instance, if you lift a barbell weighing 100 pounds overhead 10 consecutive times, you have performed 10 repetitions or reps with the weight.

Research has shown that the greatest gains in muscular strength occur when training with loads that fall in your 2 RM to 10 RM range (see Figure 7.1). RM stands for **repetitions maximum** and the number before the RM refers to the number of repetitions you can perform. For example a 2RM load is very heavy and as a result, it can only be lifted twice. A 10RM load is lighter and can be lifted 10 times but is too heavy to lift eleven times. On the other hand, if you are more interested in developing muscular endurance, then training with a 20RM weight load would be best. Most fitness enthusiasts train for moderate increases in both strength and endurance and thus lift weights that fall in the 10RM to 15RM range (see Figure 7.1).

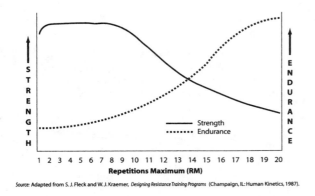

Source: Adapted from S. J. Fleck and W. J. Kraemer, *Designing Resistance Training Programs* (Champaign, IL: Human Kinetics, 1987).

Figure 7.1: Repetitions Continuum Scale

How long should a resistance training workout be?

Unlike cardiorespiratory training, resistance training has no ideal length of time required for each workout. The length of a training session depends on the number of muscle groups being trained, the number of **sets** and repetitions of each exercise being performed,

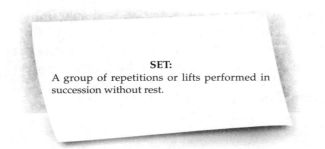

SET:
A group of repetitions or lifts performed in succession without rest.

and the amount of rest taken between each set or exercise. A resistance training program for the average person may take only 45 minutes, while for a trained athlete it may take 90 minutes. The time taken between sets and/or exercises, more than any other factor, affects the length of the workout. Unfortunately, again, there is no ideal rest interval between sets or exercises. The rest time taken between sets should be long enough for you to feel recovered before starting your next set, perhaps 2 to 3 minutes. The amount of rest taken when changing to another exercise can be shorter, perhaps 1 to 2 minutes, if you structure your program so that you train opposite muscle groups in sequence. For example, after finish-

ing the bench press, you would perform seated rows or after performing biceps curls you would train the triceps. Obviously, putting a little thought into the order in which you perform exercises can affect your training time.

A WAY OF LIFE

The typical resistance training program will last about 45 to 60 minutes depending on the number of sets and exercises performed and the rest taken between them.

How often should I resistance train?

You must get adequate rest between workouts to enable your muscles to recover before the next training session. Generally, at least 48 hours between workouts is recommended, which means no more than three training sessions for the same muscles per week. Research shows this frequency of training can lead to significant increases in muscle strength, especially in untrained individuals. It should be noted that there is growing evidence that as little as two training sessions per week can be just as effective. Resistance training only twice per week allows for greater recovery time between workouts and gives you more training time for improving other components of physical fitness.

A WAY OF LIFE

Training the same muscles 2 to 3 times per week with a minimum of 48 hours between workout sessions is adequate for improving muscular strength and endurance.

WHAT ARE SOME OTHER RESISTANCE TRAINING GUIDELINES?

In addition to the training specifics, keep in mind the following simple guidelines to make training even safer and more effective.

Should I breathe or hold my breath while performing resistance exercises?

When resistance training, avoid holding your breath. Very often when lifting weights, people inhale deeply and then begin holding their breath, in what is known as the **Valsalva maneuver**. This maneuver causes dangerous fluctuations in blood pressure, with an initial rapid increase in blood pressure followed by a

VALSALVA MANEUVER:
The act of holding one's breath when lifting weights. The Valsalva maneuver causes dangerous fluctuations in blood pressure and should not be performed.

rapid decrease. In fact, if you continue to hold your breath for too long, you can suffer **weight lifter's blackout**. This occurs because the heart is not able to pump enough blood to the brain.

WEIGHT LIFTER'S BLACKOUT:
Passing out during weight lifting due to performing the Valsalva maneuver (breath holding).

Thus it is important to make a conscious effort to breathe while lifting. A rule of thumb is to "exhale with effort." That is, you want to exhale when lifting the weight or moving the weight stack upwards against gravity and inhale on the return phase when the weight or weight stack is being lowered.

A WAY OF LIFE

Avoid holding your breath while performing resistance exercises. Remember to "exhale with effort".

How quickly should I try to move the weight when lifting?

There is no universally accepted speed of movement to use when strength training. As a general rule, the lifting phase of the repetitions should be faster than the lowering phase. One school of thought suggests that if it takes two seconds to lift the weight, it should take about four seconds to lower it back to the starting position. Regardless of the lifting speed you decide to use, it is critical that the movement be controlled at all times. No bouncing or use of momentum during the performance of the exercise should occur. Bouncing movements do nothing to improve your strength, and more importantly, can lead to serious injury.
[Insert Illustration 7.1]

It is critical that the lifting movement be controlled at all times.

A WAY OF LIFE

When performing resistance exercises, it is critical that movements be controlled at all times. No bouncing or jerky-type movements allowed.

When performed correctly, strength training can actually improve flexibility. The key is to use proper form and move the resistance through the full range of motion. All too often individuals can't move the resistance through the full range because it's too heavy or they don't know how to perform the exercise correctly. Using slightly less resistance and taking a little time to learn how to perform the exercise correctly will go a long way toward ensuring the success of your program. Seeking help from individuals certified by the National Strength and Conditioning Association (i.e. Certified Strength Conditioning Specialist or Certified Personal Trainer), the American Council on Exercise (i.e. Certified Personal

Trainer), or the American College of Sports Medicine (i.e. Health/Fitness Instructor or Certified Personal Trainer) is good advice.

Should I keep records of my resistance training?

You should keep accurate training records using a training log like the one shown in Figure 7.2. For your convenience we have included resistance training logs in Appendix C. Keeping track of training resistances, exercises, sets, repetitions, and machine settings is a great way to save time and to keep yourself motivated. Frequently a person's perspective of how far they have come or how much they have gained is lost over time. Keeping records maintains your perspective by allowing you to look back and see how far you have come. Needless to say, seeing the payoff of your labor serves as an excellent motivator to maintain your lifelong fitness program.

How can I minimize my risk for injury while resistance training?

The best way to avoid injuries when resistance training is to maintain correct technique while performing the exercises. It is beyond the scope of this book to discuss specific techniques for all the resistance exercises that can be performed. As a result, we strongly recommend that you consult with a certified fitness professional if you have any doubts about your technique. Bouncing weights off your body or the weight stack, using momentum to help you perform a lift, and contorting your body into different configurations to lift a weight are all excellent ways to injure yourself. It's important to remember not to sacrifice form for weight.

BODY REGION & EXERCISE USED		SET 1	SET 2	SET 3	COMMENTS (i.e. Machine Settings & Adjustments, etc.)
1: Hips and Front of Thighs	Weight				
	Reps				
2: Back of Thighs	Weight				
	Reps				
3: Chest	Weight				
	Reps				
4: Upper Back	Weight				
	Reps				
5: Shoulders	Weight				
	Reps				
6: Lower Back	Weight				
	Reps				
7: Abdominals	Weight				
	Reps				
8: Side of Trunk	Weight				
	Reps				
9: Front of Upper Arms	Weight				
	Reps				
10: Back of Upper Arms	Weight				
	Reps				
11: Front of Lower Leg	Weight				
	Reps				
12: Back of Lower Leg	Weight				
	Reps				

Figure 7.2: Resistance Training Recording Sheet

Another safety tip is to train with a partner, particularly if you are lifting barbells and dumbbells. A training partner can serve as a **spotter** to help you complete a repetition, to assist in lifting weights off racks, or to hand them to you once you are ready to begin. A training partner can also be an excellent source of motivation.

SPOTTER:
A person who assists with safety, checks form, and encourages the lifter performing a resistance exercise.

Always perform an active warm-up of the exercise you are about to perform. An active warm-up involves performing a practice set of the specific exercise using a light weight (approximately 50 percent of your training weight). Doing so gives you a practice run in the exercise and helps warm up the specific muscles and joints about to be worked.

Finally, make sure your strength training program is balanced. In other words, train opposing muscle groups equally. Avoid the temptation to exclusively train your favorite muscles. The musculoskeletal system works by having muscle groups oppose one another. For example the biceps muscle of the upper arm bends the elbow while the triceps muscle straightens the elbow. It is important to maintain a strength balance between opposing muscles since imbalances can lead to injury.

DO I NEED ANY SPECIAL CLOTHING, ACCESSORIES, OR EQUIPMENT?

If you have flipped through any fitness magazines lately, you are undoubtedly aware of the many ads pushing various types of training apparel and equipment. How much, if any, of this do you actually need for resistance training? No special clothing is required for resistance training because it is generally performed in the controlled environment of a health club, gym, or home. The most important factor is whether the clothing is comfortable

and nonrestrictive. The clothes can range from comfortable sweatpants and T-shirts to the more expensive Lycra warm-up outfits or Spandex shorts. Although the type of clothing worn is not of utmost importance, wearing it is. Resistance training without shirts can be dangerous and unsanitary. The vinyl upholstery covering most weight benches and pads on machines becomes quite slick when wet, which can lead to injuries. Furthermore, it is extremely unpleasant to perform an exercise on a bench soaked with someone else's sweat. Be courteous. Wear clothing that is absorbent and/or carry a towel around with you to wipe down the pads and benches when you are done.

What kind of shoes do I need for resistance training?

No special shoes are required for resistance training other than they should not be open toed (i.e. no sandals or flip-flops). A closed toe box helps to protect your feet from injury (i.e. stubbed toes or bruises from falling weights) and to prevent the spread of certain infections. The shoes should have a firm sole and give good lateral and arch support. Although running shoes are okay, tennis, basketball-type, or cross-training shoes are best.

Do I need to buy a lifting belt and any other accessories?

Some people consider wrist and knee wraps, wrist straps, gloves, chalk, and lifting belts to be standard equipment needed for resistance training. Not so. Except for gloves, you don't need any of this equipment. In fact, we discourage use of lifting accessories. Wraps, straps, and belts are frequently used more as crutches to lift additional weight than they are for safety. Most fitness professionals recommend that a resistance training program should involve loading the muscles within the limits of good exercise technique without dependence on joint wraps (knee and wrist). Doing so ensures that the muscles and the supportive connective tissues are challenged by the training and adapt in a balanced manner.

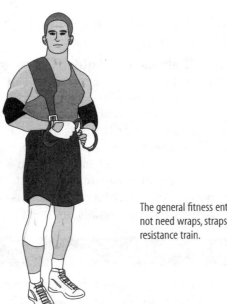

The general fitness enthusiast does not need wraps, straps, or belts to resistance train.

Likewise, except in instances when training with near maximal loads (i.e. weights that can only be lifted one to five times), lifting belts are not recommended. Lifting belts assist the abdominal and oblique muscles in squeezing in on the abdomen to increase intra-abdominal pressure. This increased intra-abdominal pressure helps to redistribute some of the loading off of the vertebral column when lifting. However, if lifting belts are always relied upon for support during training, the abdominal muscles will not be challenged to get stronger. The end result is an imbalance in strength between the muscles of the arms and legs versus the abdominal muscles that help support the spine. This increases the risk for injury when performing lifting activities without a belt, since the weaker abdominal muscles by themselves may not be able to support the spine adequately. Obviously the consequences can be costly and painful. Remember, keep the use of lifting belts to an absolute minimum.

WHAT ARE THE DIFFERENT TYPES OF RESISTANCE TRAINING EQUIPMENT?

Free weights are the most common type of resistance training equipment. Free weights include barbells, dumbbells, bars, and weight plates. This equipment is relatively inexpensive and can be purchased at most sporting goods stores. Free weights are frequently sold in sets that include a steel bar that is five to seven feet long, various weight plates ranging from 2.5 pounds to 45 pounds each, and collars for holding the weight plates on the bar. A 310-pound set of weights generally sells for about $200. Dumbbells are the small weighted handles that are individually held in each hand. They range in size from 1 to 100-plus pounds and are generally sold by the pound. Their price ranges from 45 to 75 cents per pound. Consult with a fitness expert to determine which types and how much free weight equipment you need for resistance training at home.

Most high school, university, corporate, and commercial fitness centers provide not only free weights but also some resistance training machines. One advantage of such equipment is the ease with which you can change the weight loads (weight stacks are accessible from the exercise position) and adjust the equipment to suit your body size. Each piece of equipment usually has a placard mounted in a visible position with step-by-step instructions and illustrations. Most important, strength machines are safer than free weights and do not require a spotter. The smooth performance of the equipment along with its ease of use allows for quick and efficient workouts.

Home versions of these exercise machines are also available at most sporting goods stores. If you are interested in purchasing one for your home expect to spend anywhere from $1,000 to $4,500 for a good machine. You should always try before you buy any resistance training machine, making sure it adjusts to your body size and that it operates smoothly. It is wise to get a fitness expert to help you pick out the best machine for your needs. Whether you have access to free weights or machines, the principles of training (see Chapter 4) are the same. A dynamic resistance training program should systematically, progressively, and regularly impose demands on the muscles of the body in order to develop muscular strength.

A WAY OF LIFE

You should always try before you buy when it comes to resistance training equipment. A resistance training machine that is unstable, doesn't adjust to fit your body, or does not operate smoothly under heavy load should not be bought regardless of price.

WHAT ARE SOME OF THE ADAPTATIONS RESULTING FROM RESISTANCE TRAINING?

The physiological changes that occur over the course of a training period (say, six to eight weeks) are referred to as **training adaptations**. If you repeatedly challenge and stimulate your muscles in the proper manner, you will see beneficial changes in your musculoskeletal sys-

TRAINING ADAPTATION:
A physiological change within the body that occurs in response to regular physical exercise. A common training adaptation to resistance exercise is muscle hypertrophy.

tem. Besides the obvious improvement in strength and endurance, the most outwardly observable adaptation to a resistance training program is muscle hypertrophy. Muscle hypertrophy is believed to be primarily the result of enlargement of the thousands of cells that compose the muscles. Because the muscle cells are required to generate greater forces, they respond to the training by making more **contractile proteins**. These contractile proteins are directly responsible for the muscle cells' force-

CONTRACTILE PROTEINS:
The small proteins found inside muscle cells that interact with one another and are responsible for the pulling forces generated by muscle

generating capabilities. By making more contractile proteins, each muscle cell becomes larger and stronger, which in turn makes the entire muscle larger and stronger. The degree of muscle hypertrophy is affected by the intensity of training and the hormone testosterone. This is why women, who do not have high levels of testosterone, do not demonstrate the amount of hypertrophy that men do.

There is also evidence indicating that not only do the muscle cells become larger in response to resistance training but they also increase in number. This is called **muscle fiber hyperplasia**. This increase in the number of muscle cells makes the muscle bigger and stronger. These findings conflict with the long-

MUSCLE FIBER HYPERPLASIA:
An increase in the number of cells found within a muscle.

held belief that a person is born with a set number of muscle cells and that this number does not change throughout life. It should be noted that the extent to which muscle cell hyperplasia contributes to muscle hypertrophy in humans is unclear. Thus it is currently believed that individual muscle cell enlargement, rather than muscle cell hyperplasia, is the primary way in which the muscle gets larger and stronger.

Some women fear that exercising with barbells and weight machines will make them overly muscular and masculine (i.e. unfeminine). There is no scientific basis for either of these fears. First, as noted earlier, the potential for muscle hypertrophy is determined largely by testosterone levels. Testosterone levels in males are much higher than in females and, in turn, cause the larger muscles typically seen in males. Second, resistance training does not raise the overall level of testosterone in females. In other words, resistance training does not cause women to become more masculine. More and more women are enjoying the changes in body composition and shape that strength training affords them. In fact, it is not uncommon to see more women than men in the previously male-dominated weight room.

A WAY OF LIFE

Resistance training will not make women overly muscular and masculine.

While resistance training can cause some muscle enlargement it has been erroneously touted by some equipment manufacturers as a means to increase breast size. Resistance training can increase the size of the chest muscles, but it does nothing for the overlying breast tissue. Heredity, body fatness, and pregnancy are the factors that determine breast size.

WHAT EXERCISES WILL BUILD STRENGTH AND ENDURANCE?

This section examines primary exercises for the muscles of the various regions of the body. Because a variety of resistance exercises can be used to work a particular muscle, examples of some of the more common ones are shown. If you do not have access to free weights or machines, we have also included partner-assisted exercises, calisthenic-type exercises, and exercises using elastic bands. Remember, if you are working with free weights a spotter should be present. Also, for all the exercises, it is imperative that you learn correct form and technique to avoid injury. If you are unsure about your form or technique, consult a fitness professional.

A WAY OF LIFE

If you do not have access to free weights or machines, you can resistance train using partner-assisted exercises, calisthenics-type exercises, and exercises using elastic bands.

To put together a resistance training program, pick one exercise for each of the body regions and perform them in the order listed. If you are just starting, perform a light warm-up set of the exercise followed by a 1-minute rest, and one training set of 10 RM. After 2 to 4 weeks you can add a second training set, and after about 8 weeks, you can add a third training set. For most people, three training sets is adequate to continue building muscular strength and endurance. A final note: Don't be afraid to periodically change resistance exercises. It adds variety to your workouts and ensures continued strength improvement.

What are Some Exercises for the Hips and Front of The Thighs?

Technique tips:

1. When performing squats and lunges, keep your lower back extended so that the normal curvature is maintained (do not round your low back) throughout the exercise.
2. When performing squats and leg presses, place your feet shoulder width apart, with you toes turned out slightly.
3. Do not allow your knees to move forward past your toes.
4. Do not exceed a 90-degree bend in the knees.

Seated leg presses

Squats

Partner hamstring curls

Wall squats

Partner leg presses

Lying hamstring curls

What Are Some Exercises For The Back Of The Thighs?

Technique tips:

1. When performing the prone hamstring curl exercises:
   a.) Do not allow your lower back to arch.
   b.) Do not hyperextend your neck by looking up. Rest your head on the bench or keep looking down.

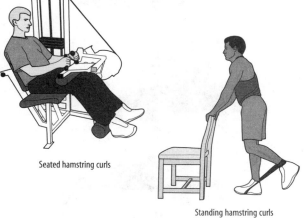

Seated hamstring curls

Standing hamstring curls

What Are Some Exercises For The Chest?

Technique tips:

1. Position your hands about shoulder width apart.
2. When using a chest press machine, adjust the machine so that the handles are about nipple level.
3. When using a barbell, do not bounce the bar off your chest.
4. Do not arch your lower back to complete the lift.

Seated chest flys

Bench presses

Push-ups

Dumbbell chest presses

Lying dumbbell flys

Seated chest presses

Partner push-ups

Push-ups with elastic band

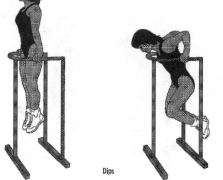
Dips

One arm dumbbell rows

Seated cable rows

What Are Some Exercises For The Upper Back?

Technique tips:

1. Concentrate on squeezing your shoulder blades together at the top position.
2. Do not arch your lower back in order to complete the lift.

Pull-ups

Lat pulldowns

Seated lat pullovers

Straight arm lat pulldowns

Seated rows

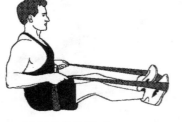
Seated rows with elastic band

Partner seated rows

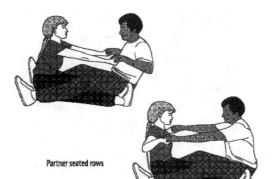
One arm cable pulldowns

What Are Some Exercises for the Shoulders?

Technique tips

1. When performing the shoulder press, do not arch your lower back to complete the lift.

Partner lateral deltoid raises

Dumbbell lateral deltoid raises

Lateral deltoid raises

Seated shoulder presses

Dumbbell upright rows

Barbell upright rows

What Are Some Exercises For The Lower Back?

Lower back pain is a common complaint of many men and women. In general, the causes of backaches include poor posture caused by weak abdominal muscles, improper body mechanics, inactivity, excess body fat, and weak lower-back muscles. In many cases, appropriate exercises can eliminate the cause of back pain. According to statistics, about 80 percent of back pain is due to muscular weakness or inflexibility. Ruptured (herniated) vertebral disks account for less than five percent of all cases of back pain

Technique tips:

1. Do not arch (i.e. hyperextend) your lower back.
2. Do not hyperextend your neck.

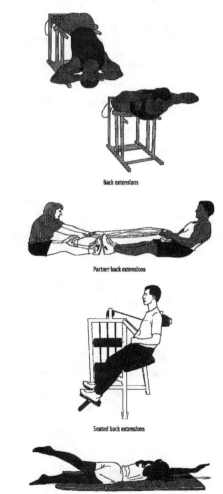

Lateral deltoid raises with elastic band

Upright rows with elastic band

Back extensions

Partner back extensions

Seated back extensions

Lying alternating limb lifts

What Are Some Exercises For The Abdominal Region?

Whether you use weights or not, exercises for developing abdominal strength and endurance are a must in every physical fitness program. The abdominal muscles play a prominent role in maintaining correct posture and thus preventing lower-back pain. They also help stabilize the torso when performing work with the arms or legs. By stabilizing the torso, strong abdominals enable the muscles of the upper and lower extremities to generate more force. More force generated at the extremities can mean running faster, jumping higher, and changing directions quicker. It is no wonder that many coaches call the abdominal region the body's **center of power**.

CENTER OF POWER:
The muscles of the mid-region of the body (i.e. lower back and abdominal region) that are important in stabilizing the spine.

Technique tips:

1. Avoid pulling on the back of your head with your arms when performing crunches.
2. Do not do abdominal work with straight legs.
3. Do not arch your lower back off the mat at the end of each crunch.
4. Concentrate on keeping the lower back pressed against the floor or mat.

Crunches

Seated crunches

Cable pull crunches

Crunches with roller

Low abdominal curl-ups

What Are Some Exercises For The Side Of The Trunk?

Technique tips:
1. Avoid ballistic, twisting type of movements.

Twisting abdominal crunches

Oblique side bends

Side lying oblique crunches

Oblique side bends with elastic band

Hanging oblique crunches

Side lying oblique crunches with roller

What Are Some Exercises For The Front Of The Upper Arms?

Technique tips:

1. When performing arm curls, avoid arching your lower-back to complete the lift.

Preacher arm curls

Standing barbell bicep curls

Standing dumbbell curls

Partner bicep curls

Bicep curls with elastic band

Seated bicep curls

Arm pulls

Lying dumbbell tricep extensions

Seated dumbbell tricep extensions

Partner tricep extensions

Cable tricep extensions

Seated tricep extensions

Tricep pressdowns with elastic band

What Are Some Exercises For The Back Of The Upper Arms?

Technique tips:
1. When performing triceps press-downs, keep your abdominal muscles tight to prevent arching of the lower back.
2. When performing lying triceps extensions, keep your elbows pointing straight up towards the ceiling. Do not let them flare out.

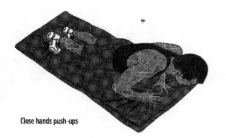
Close hands push-ups

What Are Some Exercises For The Back Of The Lower Leg?

Technique Tips:
1. When performing standing calf raises, do not lock out your knees. Keep a slight bend in your knees to prevent overstressing the knee ligaments.
2. Avoid bouncing-type movements by keeping the up and down phases of the exercise slow and controlled.

What Are Some Exercises For The Front Of The Lower Leg?

Technique Tips:
1. Keep the exercise movement isolated at your ankles by not twisting your body or changing the position of your hips.
2. Avoid rapid, bouncing-type movements to prevent the straps or elastic bands from slipping off the top of your foot.

Standing calf raises

Seated calf raises

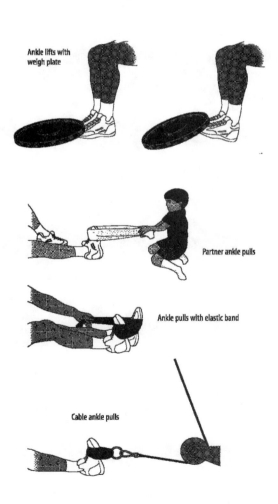
Ankle lifts with weigh plate

Partner ankle pulls

Ankle pulls with elastic band

Cable ankle pulls

Single leg calf raises

Single leg calf raises with dumbbell

SUMMARY

The benefits of resistance training are impressive. Research indicates that bones are both stronger and healthier when subjected to sufficient intensity of resistance training. Improved body composition (increased lean body mass) has always been recognized as a major benefit of resistance training programs. The development and maintenance of strength and muscular endurance helps you to be more energetic throughout your daily activities. Your posture is improved, and lifting, carrying, and moving heavy objects is easier. People with strong abdominal and back muscles tend to experience less lower-back discomfort. A regular program of strength building activities is highly motivating when it results in a firm, lean appearance. Also, people who possess good muscle strength, as well as balance and flexibility, tend to be less prone to injury during physical activity. Even walking, climbing stairs, or just sitting can be less traumatic to the body if you have well-trained muscles. All things considered, possessing a good level of strength and muscular endurance is a necessity if you want to lead a robust, active life.

When you combine strength training exercises with the exercises for cardiorespiratory endurance (Chapter 6) and flexibility (Chapter 8), you have the ingredients for developing a personalized program that will not only get you in shape but help you maintain excellent fitness and health. Remember that a safe, reasonable, and effective program will help you feel better, look better, and function better.

Improving Flexibility

8

As we age, a substantial number of us lose the ability to bend, reach, and rotate as a result of sedentary lifestyles and lack of focus on **flexibility**. In the physical fitness world, flexibility refers to the ability of a joint to move through

> **FLEXIBILITY:**
> The ability to move a joint through its fullest possible range of motion.

its fullest possible range of motion. This chapter deals with the fitness component of flexibility and offers ways to improve the range of motion at many of the body's joints. Read the following questions and after each one formulate the answer in your mind. If you don't know the answer, then read the chapter with the intent of finding the answer. If you did answer the question, then read to make sure your answer is correct and not a misconception you have about flexibility.

- If I stretch regularly will I stay injury-free?
- Can stretching make my muscles long and lean?
- Why is optimal range of motion at a joint important?
- How often can I stretch?
- How do I know I am stretching far enough?

WHAT ARE THE BENEFITS OF IMPROVING FLEXIBILITY?

Flexibility exercises, specifically **stretches**, aid in improving range of motion at joints by decreasing tension in muscles and connective tissues. When you engage in fitness activities such as those for cardiorespiratory endurance your trunk and limbs certainly move through a greater range of motion than if you just sat all day. However, even these moderate ranges of motion stop short of maximizing your flexibility. Stretches performed correctly and regularly optimize range of motion for specifically targeted joints. When joints are more mobile, muscles can do their job of moving us through space with increased efficiency and comfort.

> **STRETCHES:**
> Flexibility exercises that decrease tension in muscles and connective tissues, thus increasing range of motion at joints.

While flexibility exercises are designed to maximize a joint's range of motion, there are certain things stretching can not do. Contrary to long-held opinion, stretching has not been shown conclusively to prevent injuries or reduce muscle soreness. Similarly false is the myth that stretching can permanently 'elongate' your muscles, giving you a lean, sleek appearance. If, in fact, the act of stretching did this, what about the bones to which the muscles are attached? Since bones do not elongate when stretched, these longer, leaner muscles would simply hang off of the bones!

Regardless of any shortcomings, many people stretch simply because it feels great! During relaxation sessions that incorporate stretching to overcome tight muscles and connective tissues, your body becomes more at ease. Combined with deep breathing, stretching can contribute to stress reduction and a release of tension.

Additionally, stretching all the major muscle groups helps reduce flexibility imbalances caused by using muscle groups on one side of the trunk or limbs more than the others. Frequently these flexibility imbalances, along with strength imbalances, lead to pain or injury. A common example is the combination of tight lower back muscles plus weak abdominal muscles. The frequent result of this imbalance is lower back pain. One common approach to reducing lower back pain includes a combination of stretches for lower back and hip flexor muscles, strengthening exercises for lower back and abdominal muscles, plus posture education. While stretching may not be the definitive answer to injury prevention, developing the fullest safe range of motion for all joints enables the body to move more freely during exercise and play.

A WAY OF LIFE

Stretching regularly may enhance your entire conditioning program by allowing your movements to be at their fullest possible range of motion.

WHAT ARE THE TRAINING SPECIFICS REGARDING FLEXIBILITY EXERCISE?

In this chapter we will present a sequence of stretches that will develop flexibility of all the major muscle groups. Increasing the range of motion of all the major joints in your body requires you to perform stretches that specifically target the muscles and connective tissues crossing those joints. If your goal is to improve your overall flexibility for balanced fitness, in-

corporate all 15 stretches described in this chapter. It is also acceptable to focus on a smaller number of body parts at the start. In order to avoid flexibility imbalances and possible injuries in the future, introduce stretches for the opposing muscle groups as soon as possible.

What Is The Best Type of Exercise To Improve Flexibility?

Athletes who move their entire bodies in a wide variety of directions, positions and angles on a regular basis may not focus much time on structured stretching. Their daily activities and routines may already maximize their joint flexibility. Weight lifters moving resistance through a full range of motion in a safe, controlled manner may not need to perform actual stretches for those particular muscles. They may wish to stretch those muscles at a different joint angle or concentrate on stretching muscles they don't normally exercise. **Static stretching** has been proven very effective for general flexibility. This means you move slowly to the stretch position and hold when you reach the point of slight discomfort. ***Notice the word 'pain' is not used***

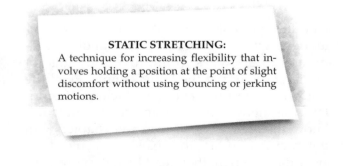

STATIC STRETCHING:
A technique for increasing flexibility that involves holding a position at the point of slight discomfort without using bouncing or jerking motions.

here! For improvements in general flexibility, avoid bouncy, ballistic movements. **Ballistic stretching** may impose sudden strains on the

BALLISTIC STRETCHING:
A technique for increasing flexibility that involves bouncing and momentum and is generally not recommended for the average fitness participant.

muscles and connective tissues involved and trigger reflexes that actually oppose the desired stretching.

How Far Should I Go When Stretching?

Overstretching, especially done with rapid movements, can lead to injury. However, the overload principle dictates that in order to improve flexibility, you have to ask your body to

move to a point just slightly beyond what is normally comfortable. Therefore, during static stretching move your trunk or limbs to a posture that safely puts the muscles and connective tissues being stretched at their greatest possible length. Never stretch to the point of pain, just to slight discomfort. Focus on relaxing as you hold the stretch. If you exhale as you move into the stretch position and then continue normal breathing as you hold, you should experience a release of tension and a sense of calm.

How Long Should I Hold My Stretches?

Once you reach the point of slight discomfort with a static stretch, hold this position for at least 20 seconds. Your muscles and connective tissues would benefit greatly from holding longer, especially if the joints are unusually inflexible. While it is perfectly acceptable to hold a stretch as long as you want, in order to get anything out of the stretch it must constantly be held at the point of slight discomfort. As you hold a stretch you may find that your trunk or limb loosen up considerably. When this happens, continue stretching at ever-increasing distances to maintain that slight discomfort.

How Often and When Should I Stretch?

Unlike training for the other physical fitness components, there is no limit to how often you can perform stretching exercises. If stretching is performed correctly you do not run the risk of overuse injuries or not recovering from a previous stretching session. We recommend that stretching be performed at least 3 days per week for general flexibility and daily to see the greatest improvements.

As discussed in Chapter 5, fitness workouts should begin with a warm up consisting of low-intensity continuous activity. It is important to gradually increase body temperature, heart and breathing rates, and blood flow to the working muscles before shifting into the more vigorous conditioning part of your workout. After 3 to 5 minutes of such movements either perform stretches for all major muscle groups or focus on specific muscles that feel particularly tight. If you feel loose enough to move your trunk and limbs through their full range of motion for your conditioning segment, stretching can take place at other points in the workout. Stopping to stretch after you have warmed up for a cardiorespiratory endurance workout will necessitate an additional

mini warm-up to return your heart rate to your target range before beginning the vigorous conditioning segment. It may be more advantageous to stretch after your cool down when you are not concerned with maintaining your

> **MINI WARM-UP:**
> The additional period of light exercise needed to gradually increase heart and breathing rates and muscle temperature if an exerciser has stopped to stretch after an initial cardiorespiratory endurance exercise warm up.

target heart rate range. Post-cool down is also a time when your muscles and connective tissues are warmer and more pliable. Stretching here when you are more relaxed, not keyed up and ready to move may prove optimal.

A WAY OF LIFE

Stretches performed following your cool down may be most beneficial due to the warmth and pliability of your muscles and connective tissues at this time.

If you are performing muscular strength and endurance exercises, heart rate is not an issue. In this instance, stretching between sets makes the most of your rest periods. You are still able to rest while you stretch, and this method saves you time by eliminating the need to stretch at the end of the workout. Your between-sets stretches may also improve the range of motion for joints involved in the particular strength/endurance exercise being performed.

Consider impromptu stretching whenever you get a chance (ie., while watching TV or talking on the phone) or whenever you feel your body tightening up (ie., during a long car or plane trip). Once you become familiar with your muscles and their particular stretches, you may find yourself unconsciously stretching at any point during the day as your body dictates.

ARE THERE ANY STRETCHES I SHOULD AVOID?

Obviously even the best flexibility program can be injurious if the stretches are performed incorrectly. Additionally, careful re-evaluation of certain traditional stretches that have been performed for years show them to provide a high risk of injury for most people. When there is a safer substitute for a risky stretch we recommend relying on that one. The following represent some examples of riskier exercises to avoid. As you will see, most of the problems with these stretches relate to the potential for overstretching and moving joints in ways for which they are not designed. For each contraindicated stretch we have suggested an alternative that is less risky.

Yoga Plough: The original purpose of this exercise was to stretch the muscles of the upper and lower back and hips. It is possible that this exercise can injure the nerves and vertebral discs in the neck and back region by using body weight to forcibly stretch the muscles. A safe alternative is the lower back and hip stretch.

Yoga plough

Don't

Hurdler Stretch: This old standby has been used for years, especially by track athletes. It still may be appropriate for the highly trained hurdler or sprinter, but it puts abnormal stresses on the inner side of the knee of the rear bent leg. These knee ligaments would be safer with the athlete performing the standing or lying quadriceps stretch.

Hurdler stretch

Don't

Toe touching

Don't

Deep Knee Bends: It was common years ago to see football athletes waddling around performing deep knee bends or stretches in the full squat position. Who knows how many knee injuries have resulted from this forcible bending of the knee joint with full body weight? The standing or lying quadriceps stretch and the inner thigh stretch are recommended alternatives.

Neck Hyperextension or Full Neck Circles: When you drop your head back, either alone or as part of a circling motion, you risk damaging the nerves and vertebral discs of the neck. This is especially true of fast, uncontrolled neck circles. Safer alternatives are the rear and side neck stretches.

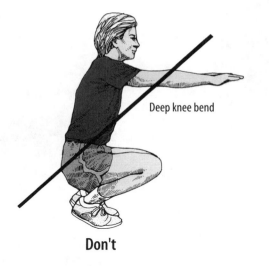

Deep knee bend

Don't

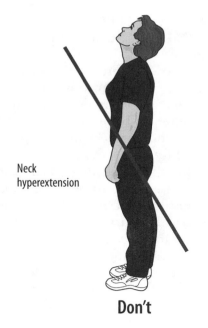

Neck hyperextension

Don't

Toe Touching: For years toe touching or 'windmills' were standard recommended daily exercises. Bending at the waist from a standing position and using upper body weight and bouncing to touch the toes puts extensive stress on the ligaments and vertebral discs of the back. The hamstring stretch and lying hip twist and gluteal stretch are safe alternatives

DO I NEED SPECIAL CLOTHING OR EQUIPMENT FOR STRETCHING?

A major plus of stretching is that it requires no special clothing or equipment. It goes without saying that loose fitting or stretchy clothing will allow you to move most comfortably in your full range of motion. Exercises performed in the lying position may benefit from an exercise mat if a carpet or rug is not available. While stretching outdoors, use a tree for balance and the grass as a soft mat.

For individuals with near-optimal flexibility and for whom money is no object, range of motion may be enhanced with the use of commercial stretching aids. For example, plastic devices that look like rockers fit under your feet to help stretch your calf muscles and Achilles tendon. A rope and pulley system that fits over your door is designed to stretch hamstrings, quadriceps and upper body muscles. You may choose to use household items such as towels or ropes to enhance the range of motion of your stretches. Perhaps the cheapest stretching aid is a partner trained to take your trunk or limb to the point of slight discomfort and either hold or give it resistance. This does require clear communication between partners and a knowledge of safe support positions.

WHAT ARE SOME FLEXIBILITY EXERCISES I CAN PERFORM?

The following are stretches for all the major muscle groups. You may perform them in any order you desire. You may remember the flow better and not omit any stretches if you begin with your neck and progress down your body. Stretches can be performed either standing, sitting, or kneeling unless stated otherwise. For standing upper body exercises, knees should be slightly bent. Feet should be shoulder-width apart with the upper body aligned with the pelvis. Remember, stretching should be smooth and controlled. Hold each stretch for a minimum of 20 seconds or longer, and perform the stretch as many times as needed to see a change in your range of motion.

Rear and Side Neck Stretches

Purpose:
To stretch muscles at the rear and sides of the neck
Procedure:
1. Press both shoulders down and main-

tain this depressed position throughout the stretching.
2. Lower your chin toward the middle of your chest and hold 20 seconds.
3. Move your chin approximately 2 inches to the right, continuing to aim it downward. Hold 20 seconds before repeating the stretch approximately 2 more inches to the right. Hold for 20 seconds and then continue in a path toward your right shoulder, holding every 2 inches for 20 seconds.
4. When you reach your right shoulder, hold 20 seconds.
5. Rotate your head to a face-front position and lower your right ear towards your right shoulder. Hold 20 seconds.
6. Lift your head and repeat steps 1-5 moving toward your left shoulder.

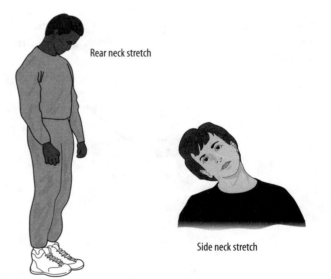

Rear neck stretch

Side neck stretch

Middle and Rear Shoulder Stretch

Purpose:
To stretch muscles in the middle and rear of the shoulder
Procedure:
1. Stand with your right arm extended straight out to your side, thumb up and palm forward. Maintain this thumb-up position throughout the stretch.
2. Bring right arm across your body in front of your chest. With left hand just

above right elbow, gently pull your right arm further across your body and hold 20 seconds.
3. Do not rotate trunk. If needed for comfort, rotate your head left to look at your right hand.
4. Repeat with left arm.

Middle-shoulder stretch

Upper Back and Rear Shoulder Stretch

Purpose:
To stretch muscles of the upper back and rear of the shoulder
Procedure:
1. Extend arms in front of your chest and cross one over the other, rotating so that palms face each other. Interlock fingers.

Upper back and rear-shoulder stretch

2. Lower your chin toward your chest.
3. Reach arms forward as far as possible, moving shoulder blades away from each other and hold 20 seconds.

Chest and Front Shoulder Stretch

Purpose:
To stretch muscles of the chest and front of the shoulder
Procedure:
1. Reach behind your trunk with both hands and interlock fingers. Keep palms facing each other and elbows slightly bent throughout the stretch. For some people this is as far as a safe stretch should go.
2. Lift arms upwards, aiming for a position horizontal to the ground. Hold 20 seconds.
3. Do not lean forward.

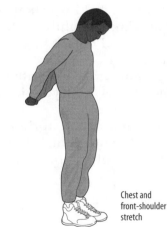

Chest and front-shoulder stretch

Triceps Stretch

Purpose:
To stretch back of upper arm and shoulder
Procedure:
1. Lift right arm straight up. Bend the elbow.
2. Place fingers and palm of right hand on right shoulder.
3. Lower chin to chest.
4. Use your left hand to gently pull your right elbow toward the left. Hold 20 seconds.
5. Repeat with left arm.

Triceps stretch

Side Stretch

Purpose:
To stretch side of trunk
Procedure:
1. Stand with feet at least shoulder width apart and knees slightly bent.
2. Place left hand on left thigh or hip for support.
3. Lift up right arm in line with your right ear and lean as far to your left as possible. Hold 20 seconds.
4. Return trunk to the upright position and repeat to the right, beginning with your left arm lifted up.

Side stretch

Abdomen Stretch

Purpose:
To stretch abdominal muscles
Procedure:
1. Lie face down on the floor, hands placed just outside your shoulders.
2. Look at the floor and maintain that head position throughout the stretch (not only is it safer for your neck, it also allows you to see how high your trunk has lifted).
3. Begin to straighten elbows, arching back slightly. *Important*: if the arching of the back is painful, either lower your trunk to a more comfortable position or eliminate this stretch.
4. Stretch only to the point where your navel begins to leave the floor. Hold 20 seconds. Pelvis should maintain contact with the floor throughout the stretch.

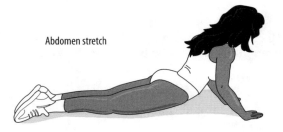
Abdomen stretch

Lower Back and Hip Stretch

Purpose:
To stretch lower back muscles, gluteals (buttocks), and hamstrings at the hip joint
Procedure:
1. Lie on back with legs softly bent at the knees.
2. Bend right knee, grasp behind the thigh in a hugging motion, and pull towards chest, while keeping head on floor.
3. Keep left leg softly bent and hold 20 seconds.
4. Return right leg to the floor and repeat with left leg.

Lower-back and hip stretch

Lying Hip Twist and Gluteal Stretch

Purpose:
To stretch spinal, outer hip, and gluteal muscles

Procedure:
1. Lie on your back with legs straight. Hold your arms out in line with your shoulders to form a 'T' for balance.
2. Your head does not need to turn during this stretch.
3. Cross your left leg over your right leg so that your left heel is next to your right ankle. For some people this is as far as a safe stretch should go.
4. Slowly bend your left knee and allow the heel to slide up your right leg as far as possible. Allow your trunk to twist and lower your bent left leg to rest on the floor. Your right hand can press gently downward on the thigh for additional stretch.
5. Try keeping your left shoulder on, or close to, the floor. Hold 20 seconds.
6. Slide your left leg back to the starting position and repeat on other side.

Lying hip twist and gluteal stretch

Inner Thigh Stretch

Purpose:
To stretch inner thigh muscles in the groin area

Procedure:
1. Sit with soles of feet together, knees relaxed outward.
2. Hold ankles (not toes) and slowly bring heels toward body.
3. While pressing downward with the elbows on your thighs, bend from hips as if to bring chest to feet, keeping back straight. Hold 20 seconds.

Inner thigh stretch

Hip Flexor Stretch

Purpose:
To stretch muscles on the front of the hip joint

Procedure:
1. Bend your knees and place both hands on the floor on either side of your feet.
2. Extend your left leg behind you as far as possible, resting on your toes.
3. Keep your right knee directly above your right heel.
4. Lower the front of your pelvis toward the ground (don't expect it to move very far downward). Hold 20 seconds.
5. Support yourself with hands on the floor as you switch legs and repeat on right side.

Hip flexor stretch

Standing Quadriceps Stretch

Purpose:
To stretch muscles on the front thigh
Procedure:
1. Stand on left leg, holding onto wall or other support with left hand.
2. Bend right knee and grasp right ankle with right hand, knee pointing down.
3. Bring right heel toward buttocks, maintaining a large angle between the lower and upper leg if you feel any knee pain.
4. Move the right thigh directly backward. Hold 20 seconds.
5. Repeat with the left thigh.
Note: This exercise can also be done lying on your side if no support is available or if balance is a problem.

Standing quad stretch (top) and alternate position for quad stretch

Hamstring Stretch

Purpose:
To stretch back of the thigh and calf muscles
Procedure:
1. Sit on floor with right leg extended in front and the left leg bent at knee so the sole of your foot touches the inside of the right leg.
2. Keep right kneecap facing ceiling and flex ankle so toes point straight up. Maintain this position throughout the stretch.

3. Put a slight arch in your low back (unless painful) and lean forward from hips. Hold 20 seconds.
4. Hands can remain on floor beside hips or behind the right thigh to gently pull the trunk forward. *Note*: It may be helpful to start seated on the floor with your trunk supported with a wall behind you.
5. Repeat with the left leg extended.

Hamstring stretch

Shin Stretch

Purpose:
To stretch shin muscles especially where they cross the front of the ankle joint
Procedure: (*note*: this works best without shoes)
1. Stand on your left leg, supporting yourself on a chair or on your thigh.
2. Place your right foot with the top of the foot facing the ground as far behind you as possible.
3. Gently bend both knees and lower the top of your right foot downward. Hold 20 seconds.
4. Repeat with the left leg.

Shin stretch

Calf and Achilles Tendon Stretch

Purpose:

To stretch calf muscles and Achilles tendon at/just above the heel

Procedure:

1. Stand approximately 2 feet away from a solid support (wall or tree) and place hands at shoulder level with arms outstretched.
2. Keep both feet facing forward throughout the stretch.
3. Extend your straight right leg back as far as possible while keeping the heel on the ground.
4. Bend the front left leg to allow maximum stretch. Hold 20 seconds.
5. To increase stretch to the Achilles tendon, bring your right foot forward until toes are next to your left heel.
6. Bend both legs and lower your body, keeping heels on the ground. Hold 20 seconds.
7. Switch legs and repeat both stretches for the left leg.

Note: This stretch can also be performed by placing hands on your front thigh (not kneecap) for support.

SUMMARY

The exercises described in this chapter offer a sound basis for improving and maintaining flexibility. Once you learn the correct methods of performing these stretches they can be used to increase your range of motion and allow your body to relax more fully. All physical movement becomes more comfortable and efficient.

Remember to begin each workout with some low-intensity rhythmic activity such as walking or jogging to elevate your heart rate and breathing rate. After this warm up, stretches can be performed for all muscle groups or simply those that remain particularly tight. Stretch between sets of muscle strengthening and endurance exercises for increased comfort and as a time saver. We suggest that after you cool down from your cardiorespiratory endurance workout you focus on stretching all major muscle groups. Flexibility is enhanced at this time when your muscles and connective tissues are more responsive to stretching. Combining stretching with all the other physical fitness components will help you create a complete and highly effective fitness program.

Calf stretch

Achilles stretch

9 *Improving Body Composition*

Nutrition relates to what foods we eat and how our bodies process them. Now that you understand how to develop and follow a sound exercise program, you are ready to adopt good eating habits. Whether you want to lose body fat, increase muscle mass, or a combination of the two, a basic understanding of

> **NUTRITION:**
> The study of food and how the body uses it.

nutrition will help you reach your body composition goals. In this chapter, we discuss basic nutrition facts to help you make sensible decisions that will positively affect your health and physical fitness. Each nutrient is discussed along with nutritional guidelines based on the "MyPyramid" food guide.

Weight management, or more specifically, management of body composition, is possible when energy intake from nutrients is closely balanced with the energy we expend during work, play, and rest. Small increases in energy intake or energy expenditure can cause controllable changes in the amount of weight gained or lost, respectively. Much has been written about innumerable diets and weight loss programs. Unfortunately, much of this information lacks a sound scientific basis. This chapter focuses on how regular vigorous exercise combined with a sensible eating plan can

effectively control body composition. In addition, we discuss common misconceptions about exercise and fat control and present approximate energy costs for a variety of physical activities.

Carefully read the following questions and after each one formulate the answer in your mind. If you don't know the answer, then read the chapter with the intent of finding the answer. If you feel you know the answer to a question, then read to make sure your answer is correct and not a misconception you have about nutrition and/or managing body composition.

- What are the basic nutrients in human nutrition?
- What roles do each of the basic nutrients play in our bodies?
- Where can you find information on good nutrition guidelines?
- What is meant by energy balance and why is understanding it important?
- How can you determine your total daily energy requirements?
- What role does exercise play in helping to manage body composition?
- What is the best way to lose body fat?
- What are the current recommendations for how to gain muscle mass?

WHAT ARE THE SIX BASIC NUTRIENTS?

Foods provide us with a wide variety of essential substances, or **nutrients**. There are six basic nutrients our bodies need for survival: carbohydrates, fats, proteins, minerals, vitamins, and water. The key for us nutritionally is to take in adequate amounts of each of these nutrients in order to ensure normal functioning of the body. The energy our body needs is pro-

> **NUTRIENTS:**
> The basic substances needed by the body that are provided by eating food.

vided by the first three categories of nutrients listed above: carbohydrates, fats, and proteins. These nutrients are also collectively known as the **macronutrients** because they are our source of energy and thus we need to consume

> **MACRONUTRIENTS:**
> The nutrients that provide the body with energy and thus must be consumed in large amounts on a daily basis. The macronutrients are carbohydrates, fats, and proteins.

relatively large amounts of them on a daily basis. Other nutrients like minerals, vitamins, and water are essential for life but do not provide us with energy. The following sections will provide a brief description of each of the six nutrient categories.

Eating for health is not about deprivation, but about moderation.

A WAY OF LIFE

> The energy needs of the body are met by the macronutrients: carbohydrates, fats, and proteins.

What are carbohydrates?

Carbohydrates serve as a major source of energy for the body. The breakdown of carbohydrates provides us with energy so that the cells of our bodies can function properly. For

> **CARBOHYDRATES:**
> A food substance that is the primary energy food for vigorous muscular activity; includes various sugars and starches and is found in the body in the form of glucose and glycogen.

example, without carbohydrates cells would not have enough energy to maintain and repair body tissues, nerve cells could not transmit electrical signals, and muscle cells could not contract. The carbohydrates we eat are broken down during the digestive process into simple sugars, the most important of which is **glucose.** The glucose is transported across of walls of the digestive track and enters into the blood

> **GLUCOSE:**
> A building block of the carbohydrates that we eat. Carbohydrates are broken down during digestion to form glucose, which then enters the blood stream for use by our body.

stream as **blood sugar**, which is then transported throughout the body and either used for energy or stored inside cells as **glycogen**. Glycogen is nothing more than a long chain of glucose molecules linked together and stored

> **BLOOD SUGAR:**
> The glucose concentration in the blood. The term should not be confused with refined sugar.

inside a cell. When the cell needs some energy it basically breaks off a glucose molecule from the chain and uses it.

> **GLYCOGEN:**
> The storage form of carbohydrates found in the liver and muscles.

Carbohydrates are found in many different types of foods. Excellent sources of carbohydrates include fruits and vegetables and their pure extracted juices. Equally important sources include potatoes, rice, peas, whole grain cereals (e.g., wheat, oats, corn, and rice), pasta, bread, and bagels. These food sources not only provide carbohydrates but other nutrients as well.

Carbohydrate foods like candy, jams, jellies, table sugar, honey, molasses, and concentrated syrups (like corn syrup) are high in refined sugar content and are called "empty calorie" foods because they provide energy but little or no other nutrients. Direct your focus instead on eating foods that provide a better nutrient return for the caloric investment. The consumption of refined sugars should be limited when they interfere with adequate intake of other nutrients or maintenance of proper energy balance. According to estimates, the average American consumes well over 100 pounds of refined sugar per year and the typical American diet has 25 percent or more of its calories in the form of sugar. Much of these sugars are hidden in the processed foods that we consume regularly, such as ketchup and fruit cocktail drinks.

Approximately 55 percent of the calories you eat should come from carbohydrates found in vegetables, fruits, and starchy foods. The Senate Select Committee on Nutrition and Human Needs recommends cutting your intake of refined sugar (sucrose) to about 15 percent of your total calories. This means that 40 percent of your total calories should be carbohydrates other than refined sugar. Keep in mind, however, that even though complex carbohydrates are usually considered the "good guys" in the battle of the bulge, you can eat too much of a good thing. Whenever you take in more carbohydrates than your body needs, the excess is converted to fat and stored, thus increasing body fat levels. To calculate the number of carbohydrate calories in your food, simply multiply the number of carbohydrate grams, which can be found on the nutrition label, by four.

What are fats?

Fats, similar to carbohydrates, serve as a major source of energy for the body. Fats in the foods we eat are broken down and transported via the lymph and blood to cells throughout the body. If the fats are not used for energy,

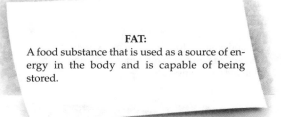

> **FAT:**
> A food substance that is used as a source of energy in the body and is capable of being stored.

they are stored in specialized fat storage cells known as **adipocytes**. These adipocytes are concentrated in the areas of the abdomen, hips,

> **ADIPOCYTE:**
> A specialized cell whose primary function is to store fat

and thighs. It's no wonder that when we gain weight these are the areas that show the most dramatic increase in size.

Fats do serve other purposes in the body besides increasing abdomen and hip size. They serve a structural role as part of the membrane wall in every cell of the body. Fats also help the nervous system to function by serving as electrical insulators. They prevent the spread of electrical impulses to areas they are not supposed to go and also help nerve cells conduct their electrical signals faster. Fats also help cushion vital organs and thus protect them from injury. Finally, as mentioned previously, fat is also a major source of energy for physical activity. To determine the number of fat calories in a food, multiply the grams of fat contained in the food by nine. Common sources of fats are meats, butter, margarine, shortening, cooking and salad oils, cream, most cheeses, mayonnaise, nuts, whole milk, eggs, and milk chocolate.

Not all fats are alike. There are two types of fats: **saturated** or **unsaturated fats**. Saturated fats come from meat, whole milk, cheese, and butter. This type of fat is generally solid at

> **SATURATED FATS:**
> A food source found in meat, whole milk, cheese, and butter. This type of fat does not melt at room temperature.

> **UNSATURATED FATS:**
> A liquid type of fat found in peanut oil and olive oil.

room temperature. However, there are some oils like palm and coconut oil, also known as the tropical oils, that are liquid at room temperature yet high in saturated fat. Saturated fats are known to raise levels of cholesterol in the bloodstream. For this reason, it is important to reduce saturated fats in your diet. No more than 30 percent of your daily calories should come from fat, with 10 percent or less coming from saturated fat sources. Replace as much of the saturated fat in your diet as possible with monounsaturated or polyunsaturated fats. These unsaturated fats tend to be in a liquid form at room temperature. The monounsaturated fats are found in canola, peanut, and olive oils. Polyunsaturated fats are found in corn, soybean, cottonseed, sunflower, and safflower oils.

A WAY OF LIFE

Fats are energy dense and thus serve as the body's energy reserves. However, no more than 30 percent of your total daily calories should come from fat and 10 percent or less should come from saturated fat sources.

What are proteins?

Proteins are the basic structural substance of every cell in the body. Protein gives structure

> **PROTEIN:**
> A food substance that provides the basic structural properties of cells and is also the source for enzymes and hormones in the body.

to bones, skin, muscle fibers, hair, fingernails, connective tissue and many other tissues. Whereas proteins serve as the structural framework, carbohydrates and fats provide the energy for the body to work and move about. Enzymes and hormones are proteins that control and regulate chemical reactions in our bodies. Specialized proteins are also present in blood in the form of clotting agents and oxygen-carrying molecules. Proteins are not significant sources of energy at rest or during physical activity. Only when carbohydrate and fat intake in the diet are low and/or when physical activity is of very long duration, such as an ultramarathon, will the body begin to breakdown and use significant amounts of proteins for energy.

The proteins we eat in our diet are broken down during the digestive process into **amino acids**, which are the basic building blocks of all proteins. The amino acids are transported from

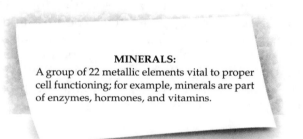

AMINO ACIDS:
The end product of the breakdown of protein.

the gut via the blood to the cells of the body. The cells take the amino acids and use them to construct the proteins they need. All of the different proteins synthesized by the cells are made up of unique combinations of different amino acids. Now you can see why it is important to eat good sources of protein that provide the body with all the different types of amino acids. Major sources of complete proteins come from foods of animal origin: meat, fish, poultry, eggs, and milk. Unfortunately protein-rich foods from animal sources are generally high in fat. Luckily there are excellent low-fat versions of these foods such as skim milk, low-fat yogurts, reduced-fat cheeses, lean meats, and some skinless poultry. Also, specific combinations of lower fat non-animal proteins such as peas, beans, and grains can provide all the necessary amino acids in your diet.

Proteins serve more of a structure role, rather than an energetic role in the body. Approximately 15% of total daily calories should come from protein sources.

Fifteen percent of your total calories should come from protein. One gram of protein equals four calories. To calculate the number of protein calories in your food, simply multiply the number of protein grams by four. If you don't want to count calories, multiply your body weight in kilograms by 0.8 to get the number of grams of protein needed per day.

What are minerals?

Minerals are essential inorganic substances that give strength to certain body tissues and assist with numerous vital functions.

MINERALS:
A group of 22 metallic elements vital to proper cell functioning; for example, minerals are part of enzymes, hormones, and vitamins.

Calcium, iodine, iron, phosphorous, magnesium, and other minerals are vitally important to the functioning of the body systems. For example, calcium is the most abundant mineral in the body and combines with phosphorus to form the bones and teeth. Calcium is also crucial for normal functioning of the muscles. Phosphorus and other minerals play essential roles in the breakdown of carbohydrates and fats for energy. Iodine is an important ingredient in thyroxin, a hormone that governs the rate of energy metabolism in the body. Iron is a key component of hemoglobin, which enables blood to carry oxygen.

Sodium, chloride, and potassium are also minerals that play a key role in controlling and regulating fluid balance in the body. These charged particles are found mainly in the fluids inside and outside the cells and are essential for the proper transmission of nerve impulses. Sodium is present in all living matter including meats, poultry, fish, and vegetables. It is also added in the processing of food as a preservative and stabilizer and for taste (in the form of table salt). The adequate intake of all the different minerals needed by the body is beyond the scope of this chapter but consultation with a nutrition specialist can help you make sure that your diet meets your mineral needs.

What are vitamins?

Vitamins, similar to minerals, are considered micronutrients. Because the cells of the body cannot form these substances, the vitamin needs of the body must be provided by the food you eat. Although only small amounts are needed by the body each day, this should not leave the impression that they are not crucial for survival. Vitamins are essential for the proper functioning of muscles, nerves, and other body systems. They, like minerals, also play a dynamic role in releasing energy from the carbohydrates, fats and proteins that we eat. Additionally, they help maintain and promote growth of body tissues.

> **VITAMINS:**
> Organic substances that perform vital functions within the cells.

Some vitamins tend to be retained within the body and stored in fat (fat-soluble vitamins). Megadose supplements of the fat-soluble vitamins may accumulate, creating toxic conditions in the body. Many vitamins, however, are transported in the fluids of the tissues and cells and are not stored (water-soluble vitamins). Any excess amounts of the water-soluble vitamins are usually excreted in the urine on a daily basis.

Is vitamin and mineral supplementation necessary?

Vitamins and minerals are collectively known as **micronutrients** because our bodies require very small amounts of them on a daily basis. The small quantities of vitamins and

> **MICRONUTRIENTS:**
> The nutrients that are needed in very small amounts by the body on a daily basis. The micronutrients are vitamins and minerals.

minerals required can be met by consuming a well-balanced diet consisting of fruits and vegetables. Unfortunately, the reality is that the vast majority of Americans do not eat a well balanced diet. There are a variety of reasons for this. Our hectic lifestyles often do not include well-planned daily meals, and we do not keep track of what we eat from meal to meal. In addition, we may not care for the taste or texture of many of the healthier foods or not take the time and effort to learn to prepare them in a more enticing way. Also, some of the better sources of specific vitamins (such as vitamin E) are high in fat and calories, which many of us are trying to reduce in our diets.

A WAY OF LIFE

While a well-balanced diet composed of nutritious whole foods is the best source for vitamins and minerals, a vitamin/mineral supplement containing 100% or less of the recommended daily values may be taken to ensure adequate micronutrient intake..

Keep in mind that eating foods containing a variety of nutrients, vitamins, and minerals is always the best option. However, if your diet is not well-balanced or you just want to make sure that you are consuming the recommended daily amounts, then taking a one-a-day vitamin/mineral tablet is okay. Some supplements tout anti-oxidant, anti-aging doses of vitamins such as A, C, and E. Research in this area is still highly controversial and thus makes any claimed benefits of these products highly questionable. The bottom-line is that supplements containing doses of any vitamins or minerals exceeding the daily value are not necessary or prudent. Always read the supplement facts label on the bottle before you buy and check that the percentages of each vitamin and mineral are not over 100%.

A WAY OF LIFE

Taking special formulation supplements containing large doses of any vitamins or minerals exceeding the daily value is not necessary or prudent.

Why is water so important?

Because nearly 60 to 70 percent of the human body is water, our need for water is second only to our need for oxygen. Water provides the medium (body fluids) for transporting nutrients and hormones throughout the body and for removing wastes from the body. Water also plays a vital role in regulating body temperature. You get water not only by drinking it directly but also from the foods you eat. Caffeinated beverages such as coffee, many teas, colas, and various other soft drinks also serve as sources of water. However, because caffeine is a **diuretic**, not all of the water ingested counts toward daily fluid intake since some is lost in urine formation.

Get into the habit of drinking water frequently throughout your day and particularly

A WAY OF LIFE

The need for water is second only to our need for oxygen in regard to survival. As a result drink at least one liter of water for every 1,000 calories expended. For most people that means drinking at least 2 liters of water per day.

DIURETIC:
A substance that when ingested causes the body to form urine. Caffeine is an example of a diuretic.

at regular intervals during your exercise sessions. Because dehydration can begin before you feel thirsty, do not rely on thirst to gauge your need for water. In general, drink at least two liters (approximately 8 cups) of water a day or 1 liter for every 1,000 calories you expend. When participating in vigorous exercise where sweating is constant and abundant, drink a cup of water every 15 minutes. If possible drink cool water, as it is more easily absorbed than room temperature water.

Get into the habit of drinking water frequently during your exercise sessions.

A WAY OF LIFE

During activities that cause sweating, don't wait until you get thirsty before you drink water. It is recommended that you drink at least one cup of water every 15 minutes.

WHAT ARE SOME BASIC GUIDELINES FOR GOOD NUTRITION?

As a general rule, your daily nutritional needs will be met by following the recommendations of the recently implemented My Pyramid Food Plan which can be found on the web at the following address: http://www.mypyramid.gov/. In short, the pyramid is divided into six different sections, each of a different width (see Figure 9.1). The different sections represent the five food groups (i.e. Grains, Vegetables, Fruits, Milk, and Meat & Beans) and the narrowest of the sections represents oils. The stairway on the left side of the pyramid indicates that daily exercise should be combined with a healthy

Source: U.S. Department of Agriculture, U.S. Department of Health and Human Services.

Figure 9.1: My Pyramid Food Plan

diet. The different sections have different widths which symbolize how much food a person should choose from each group. For example the widest sections are the Grains, Vegetables, and Milk groups, indicating that a large proportion of your diet should consist of foods from these categories of foods. The number of servings for each group vary depending upon the person. Going to the My Pyramid website noted previously can help you determine the servings you need from each.

A WAY OF LIFE

General nutritional information, along with current recommendations and guidelines can be found at the following website address: http://www.mypyramid.gov/.

While further discussion of nutritional guidelines is important for general health, it is outside the focus of this chapter which is on managing body composition. The remainder of this chapter will focus on the macronutrients (i.e. carbohydrates, fats, and proteins). It is the macronutrients that provide the body with energy. This energy is either used or stored and thus the relationship between macronutrient intake and body composition.

WHAT IS ENERGY BALANCE AND WHY IS IT IMPORTANT?

Controlling body composition is dependent upon your understanding of a very simple concept: **energy balance**. This concept states that you must balance your energy in-

ENERGY BALANCE:
A neutral energy state in which energy consumed equals the energy expended. When the body is in energy balance, body composition is maintained.

take (food consumption) with your energy output (daily energy expenditure) to keep from gaining fat weight. If you consume more energy than you expend, you are in a **positive energy state** and the excess energy will be stored as fat. Conversely, if you consume fewer calories than you expend, then you are in a **negative energy state**. In this case, the body must cover the energy deficit by resorting to its energy stores (i.e. fat). In other words, you lose fat when in a negative energy balance.

A WAY OF LIFE

Managing body composition is all about understanding the concept of energy balance. Simply stated, if "energy consumed" equals "energy expended", then body composition will be maintained.

> **POSITIVE ENERGY STATE:**
> An energy imbalance created when daily calories consumed exceed the calories expended. In a positive energy state, body weight increases usually due to gains in body fat.

> **NEGATIVE ENERGY STATE:**
> An energy imbalance created when daily calories consumed are less than the calories expended. In a negative energy state, body weight is lost usually as body fat.

If you are trying to lose fat weight, it is always important to pay attention to food serving sizes in order to achieve a negative energy state. Too often we are unaware of what constitutes 'one serving' of a particular food. We read the nutritional information on the package, noting calories and fat, yet frequently ignore the serving size on which these numbers are based. Quoted serving sizes are often much smaller than the amount of food we actually consume. Serving size must be monitored in all healthy diets, particularly those geared toward body fat reduction.

A WAY OF LIFE

Always read the nutrition facts label to determine the actual serving size of a food. Very often the amount of food we consume exceeds the actual serving size stated.

Although a negative energy state can work to reduce body fat, research studies indicate that the composition of your diet may also be an important key to keeping off fat. High levels of dietary fat and sugar tend to promote fatness due to hormonal influences caused by their ingestion. However, complex carbohy-drates and dietary fiber, when included in the diet, tend to assist in fat loss. The point is that food intake that is low in fat and simple sugars appears to be a key factor in successful fat loss and the management of a healthy body composition. For example, include such complex carbohydrates as pastas, breads, and beans and avoid simple sugars, such as those found in candies, syrups, and regular soda pop. This does not mean that you have to give up grilled pork chops and cookies and the like. It just means that you need to eat less of them. (see My Pyramid Food Plan discussed earlier).

A WAY OF LIFE

To lose body fat you must achieve a negative energy state. Diets that are low in fat and simple sugars are key to successful fat loss and the management of a healthy body composition.

HOW CAN I DETERMINE MY DAILY ENERGY REQUIREMENTS?

All of the energy found in the foods we eat is eventually released in the form of heat. By measuring the amount of heat given off when a food is burned or when we exercise, we can determine the amount of energy released from foods or the amount of energy required for physical activity, respectively. The unit of measure for heat energy is the **kilocalorie** (often called a calorie, for short).

> **KILOCALORIE:**
> The basic unit of measure for heat energy. One kilocalorie is the heat energy needed to raise the temperature of one liter of water, one degree centigrade; often called a "calorie" for short.

The energy or kilocalorie needs of the body depend on factors such as body size, body composition, age, and type and amount of daily physical activity. Your **basal metabolic** rate (BMR) plus your energy needs for daily activities combine to represent your total daily caloric requirement. BMR is the minimum level of energy required to sustain life when in a resting state. BMR is determined usually under stringent laboratory conditions by measuring the amount of oxygen consumed during a period of complete rest at least 12 hours after the last meal.

> **BASAL METABOLIC RATE (BMR):**
> The minimal level of energy required to maintain the life processes of the body during a resting state following at least 12 hours of not eating.

How does the amount of oxygen consumed help determine how many calories are required to sustain life? The oxygen consumed by your body is used to metabolize the foods we eat for energy. Therefore, **oxygen consumption** can represent the amount of energy the body is expending. Most authorities set the basal oxygen requirement of the body at 3.5

> **OXYGEN CONSUMPTION:**
> The amount of oxygen used by the body to breakdown the foods we eat for energy. The amount of oxygen consumed can be easily converted to kilocalories (i.e. 1 liter of oxygen consumed = 4.82 kilocalories).

milliliters per kilogram of body weight per minute. It has ben established that one kilogram (2.2 pounds) of body weight burns approximately 1 calorie per hour. Knowing your weight in kilograms, you can roughly estimate your BMR. A 77-kilogram (170-pound) man, for example, would use 77 calories per hour and have a BMR of about 1,848 calories / day (1 calorie/kilogram X 77 kilograms X 24 hours). To check the accuracy of this figure, we can calculate it another way since we know that one liter of oxygen consumed equals 4.82 calories. Using a BMR of 3.5 milliliters of oxy-

gen per kilogram per minute, we get a total of 77.6 calories per hour, or 1,862 calories every 24 hours, a very close agreement.

The BMR for a woman is calculated in the same manner, only with a 10 percent reduction. The 10% reduction in BMR for women compensates for the higher body fat level that women possess. Thus a 55-kilogram (121-pound) woman would utilize just under 1,200 calories a day (0.90 calories/kilogram X 55 kilograms X 24 hours).

Once you have estimated your BMR, you must add the caloric costs for the various activities performed during your day. The total represents your 24-hour caloric expenditure. Individual daily caloric expenditures vary considerably because of differences in job requirements and recreational pursuits. Table 9.1 provides an estimate of total daily caloric expenditures for men and women of different body weights and activity levels. Note that the lighter you are or the less active you are, the fewer calories you require per day.

To estimate your total 24-hour caloric needs, follow the steps presented previously for determining your BMR. Then, using Table 9.1, select the activity level that best describes your daily lifestyle. For instance, if you choose 60 percent, multiply your BMR for 24 hours by 0.6. Add the result to your BMR. The total is an estimate of your total daily caloric expenditure. In order to maintain your present body composition, your daily caloric intake should equal the daily caloric expenditure you have calculated. If you want to lose fat, you should reduce your daily intake of calories and/or increase your activity level (to burn more calories). By following the exercise recommendations provided in the previous chapters and developing sensible eating habits, you can attain your body composition goals.

> **A WAY OF LIFE**
>
> Your total daily energy (caloric) expenditure equals your BMR + the energy cost of the entire day's activities.

Table 9.1 Estimated Daily Expenditure Based on Body Weight and Activity Level* (kilocalories per 24 hours)

| | Body Weight (kg) | | | | | | | |
| | Men | | | | Women | | | |
Activity Level	60	70	80	90	50	55	60	65
40% Sedentary: (sitting and limited walking)	2,030	2,370	2,710	3,050	1,520	1,680	1,830	1,980
50% Semisedentary: (standing, walking, and limited other physical activities)	2,180	2,540	2,900	3,270	1,630	1,790	1,960	2,120
60% Light work: (working in shop or factory with limited physical exercise)	2,320	2,710	3,100	3,480	1,740	1,910	2,090	2,260
70% Heavy work: (working in construction or regular participation in intramurals, sports, or other physical activities)	2,470	2,880	3,290	3,700	1,850	2,030	2,220	2,400
80% Active: (participation in intercollegiate sports or in a vigorous daily physical fitness program)	2,610	3,050	3,480	3,920	1,960	2,150	2,350	2,550

*Calculations are based on a basal oxygen requirement of 3.5 milliliters of oxygen for each kilogram of body weight per minute and on a caloric equivalent of 4.8 calories per liter of oxygen used. (Values listed have been rounded off to the nearest 10 calories.)

WHAT ARE SOME GUIDELINES FOR ACHIEVING OPTIMAL BODY COMPOSITION?

When it comes to food, we all need the same nutrients, but in different amounts. Young people need greater quantities of food for body growth, upkeep, and energy. Men generally need more food than women, due in part to a larger percentage of lean body mass. Large people need more food than small people. However, when people overeat, that is, when they take in more calories than their daily activities use up, they gain fat. As discussed previously, intake of food in excess of our daily needs leads to overfatness. Over half of all American adults are **overfat**, with studies indicating that number is increasing.

Obesity is an extreme level of overfatness and is a major public health problem. Obesity is defined as having 25 percent or more body fat for men and 35 percent or more body fat for women. As the most prevalent form of malnutrition in the United States, obesity has far-reaching complications. It increases the risk for cardiovascular, respiratory, kidney, and gall bladder diseases, various cancers, as well as to diabetes, disorders of the bones and joints, and, for some people, emotional imbalance. It also increases the risk for complications during surgery. Obese persons are more prone to

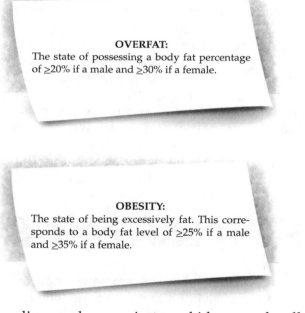

OVERFAT:
The state of possessing a body fat percentage of ≥20% if a male and ≥30% if a female.

OBESITY:
The state of being excessively fat. This corresponds to a body fat level of ≥25% if a male and ≥35% if a female.

fatigue (increasing the risk of accidents), indigestion, and constipation, and they have disproportionate numbers of aches and pains. Besides having to cope with the psychological effects of being fat, they face premature death.

Many people like to believe that some metabolic abnormality is the reason for their being obese. Most often, this is not true. Medical research does not support the notion that endocrine malfunction is the reason for obesity. Instead, evidence is accumulating that a sedentary lifestyle is the real culprit. The obese simply do not burn off the calories they consume each day, and the surplus energy is stored as fat in the body.

A consideration for those of you who are parents, or about to be, is the danger of allowing your children to become fat at an early age. Research indicates that human fat cells increase in number very rapidly in early childhood. Pediatricians are increasingly concerned over this fact. Overfeeding tends to increase the number of fat cells in the young child, making it more difficult for them to control body fat throughout his or her lifetime. To curb this potential for fatness, proper eating and exercise habits should be cultivated at an early age. Managing body fat is a lifetime affair, beginning with a parent's concern, instruction, and perhaps most importantly, role-modeling.

In determining a desirable and healthy weight, it is more important to know how fat you are rather than how much you weigh. The standard age-height-weight tables are derived from measurements of a great number of people. Although these charts enable each person to make comparisons with the average man or woman, they are often inadequate guides for figuring a healthy weight. Many athletes, low in body fat but very muscular, would be overweight according to these charts. Also, most of these age-height-weight charts allow small increases in body weight with increasing age, a practice that lacks scientific justification.

Many people low in body fat but very muscular would be considered overweight according to age-height-weight tables.

Without question, it is the proportion of fat tissue in your body (i.e. body composition), and not your scale weight, that is important. Methods have been developed for measuring body composition. Skinfold measurements using calipers, underwater weighing or the Bod Pod can be used to determine your relative fatness. Once you determine your percentage of body fat, you can refer to Table 9.2, which lists body fat norms.

Table 9.2. Norms for Body Composition

Classification	Women (% body fat)	Men (% body fat)
Desirable	18–29.9	12–19.9
Overfat	30–34.9	20–24.9
Obese	≥ 35	≥ 25

Without question, it is the proportion of fat tissue in your body (i.e. body composition), and not your scale weight, that is important in regard to health and physical fitness.

What is the role of exercise in managing body composition?

We all want to look good and feel energetic. Studies on managing body composition point to the overwhelming success of combining sensible eating with regular exercise rather than relying solely on one component. While reducing the amount of food you eat may help you lose weight, physical activity is necessary to maintain your ideal body composition. Exercise is the key to increasing your muscle mass, to burning enough calories so that you don't have to starve yourself, and to stoking your metabolism to a higher degree.

The importance of regular exercise in managing the amount of body fat and lean mass we each possess is well accepted today. Physical activity is the great variable in energy expenditure and can play a key role in controlling your body fat. To try to maintain a desirable body composition while living a sedentary life would probably mean lifelong hunger and a flabby, poorly toned body.

Trying to maintain an ideal body composition while living a sedentary lifestyle is difficult and very unhealthy.

A significant amount of the weight, as measured on a scale, that is lost from dieting alone comes from body water and lean (not fat) body tissue. Many people on a low-carbohydrate diet (e.g. Atkins Diet), which depletes stored carbohydrates, experience quick weight loss due to an associated loss of body water. They are encouraged by what they see on the scale, but in fact they are being deceived. Such crash diets often result in the loss of lean body tissue from muscles, bones, and organs. When the crash diet ends and normal eating resumes, weight is regained, mostly as fat. And when the weight is regained, the dieting often begins again. People who constantly undergo these "yo-yo diets" can become so frustrated that they simply give up.

When you start an exercise program, you can expect slight gains in muscle tissue. Even when you lose body fat, your total body weight may not change as quickly as you would expect due to this increase in lean body mass. This disappoints some people since they do not see the needle drop on their bathroom scales as much as they would expect. However, you may see a loss of inches in your girths and increased muscle tone, and your clothes may fit looser. So don't be discouraged. The right kind of weight loss is occurring. Realize that the burning off of stored fat continues if energy expenditures exceed the amount of calories you consume. To confirm your positive change in body composition, it is a good idea to reassess your percent body fat every six to eight weeks using an accepted assessment technique.

Studies have demonstrated that today's adults are increasingly less active than their counterparts in years gone by. Many people experience "creeping obesity", the gradual yet significant increase in fat over a period of years that is caused mainly by inactivity. Studies comparing obese with non-obese subjects have demonstrated that the cause of fatness is usually an inactive lifestyle, not increased food consumption. In fact, people who are active and lean tend to eat more than inactive and obese persons. The fat content of a fit individual's meals also tends to be less than that of an obese individual.

What is the best way to lose body fat?

Using exercise or diet alone to reduce body fat can prove to be difficult and time-consuming. To lose one pound of fat, you must expend 3,500 calories more than you consume. This would be the equivalent caloric expenditure of running about 35 miles! If your goal is to lose one pound per week using exercise alone, you would have to burn 500 calories more than usual every day that week (7 days X 500 calories = 3,500). Even if you exercised vigorously for 30 minutes, you would be hard pressed to burn 500 calories and would have to extend your exercise duration to 45 to 60 minutes. On the other hand, if you chose not to exercise and used diet alone, you would have to decrease your caloric intake by 500 calories per day. Since exercise is not being used, you

---

A WAY OF LIFE

To lose one pound of fat, you must expend 3,500 calories more than you consume. This is the equivalent caloric expenditure of running about 35 miles.

---

would also risk losing some lean body mass (muscle tissue). Loss of lean tissue lowers BMR and makes it hard to lose fat weight. Conversely, when you combine exercise and diet, you can maintain or even increase your lean body mass thereby helping you to achieve a healthy body composition more quickly.

Therefore, take a long-range view of your situation. Exercise daily at a reasonable caloric expenditure level of 300 calories (one you can endure), and reduce your caloric intake by 200 calories, and that 1 pound of fat loss each week is much more easily attained and maintained. Alternatively, a person could exercise longer only four days a week at 450 calories per session and combine that with a decrease in daily food intake by 450 calories for a 3,600 calorie deficit per week. The bottom line is that losing 1 to 2 pounds of body fat weekly is reasonable and achievable by most individuals. If more weight is lost, it is questionable whether it is entirely fat weight. For those anxious to lose fat, this recommendation may seem too slow. However, experience has demonstrated that if you lose body fat gradually and systematically,

---

A WAY OF LIFE

Losing 1 to 2 pounds of body fat weekly is reasonable and achievable by most individuals.

---

you are more likely to keep it off. It allows you to modify your eating habits and activity levels in sensible increments that you can live with now and in the future.

What is the best way to increase lean body mass?

Some individuals, in particular athletes, may be interested in gaining weight. However, unless the athletes are sumo wrestlers or football linemen where increased fat mass can be beneficial, most people wanting to gain weight are really wanting to gain muscle mass. Gaining muscle mass requires two things: a properly designed resistance training program (see Chapter 7) and a good diet. The resistance training provides the stimulus and the diet provides the nutrients for muscle growth.

As discussed earlier, in order to gain weight a person must enter into a positive energy balance. However, consuming too many calories will cause rapid weight gain and a proportionately greater increase in fat mass. The number of extra calories needed to support muscle growth is highly individual. Weight gain in the form of muscle is a gradual process, so increases in dietary intake should be modest in order to maximize muscle gain versus fat gain. A weight gain goal of 0.5 to 1 pound per week is generally considered appropriate. Consuming approximately 300 to 500 extra calories per day should support this rate of weight gain.

A WAY OF LIFE

A weight gain of 0.5 to 1 pound per week is generally considered appropriate. Consuming approximately 300 to 500 extra calories per day should support this rate of weight gain.

The composition of the additional calories is important. However, contrary to popular belief, protein should not make up the majority of the additional calories. The largest proportion (55% to 60%) of additional calories should come from carbohydrates with 15 to 20% coming from protein. Protein and weight gain supplements are not necessary but can make consuming the extra calories easier and more convenient, particularly for those individuals that just can't seem to eat enough food necessary to gain weight. See Table 9.3 for other nutritional tips regarding weight gain.

Table 9.3. Nutritional Tips for Weight Gain

- Avoid carbonated beverages that produce gas and bloating and the feeling of fullness
- Consume non-carbonated sports drinks instead of water during workout sessions
- Have small, frequent meals and snacks throughout the day
- Establish a time schedule and adopt strategies to prevent you from missing meals or snacks
- Consider using liquid meals or other energy dense foods for snacks
- Include a bedtime snack about 1 hour before going to sleep

SUMMARY

Food has always been a focal point of our lives. Although a necessity, eating has also been viewed as a recreational activity, something we do in leisure time for pleasure. We snack while watching television or as we study. We go out to eat at our favorite pizza parlors and fast-food restaurants. Preparation of hearty meals is a way of showing affection for others; holiday feasts and backyard barbecues are affairs we look forward to. Business transactions are frequently conducted over food and drink. The result of all this enjoyable eating can be excess fat or even outright obesity.

We live in a society that has become increasingly inactive as technology has advanced. Today, sedentary living is encouraged by the continual development of work-saving equipment and passive amusements and recreations. But the body was made to be active, and it thrives on movement and vigorous activity. An active lifestyle should be programmed into your daily living plan to counter the effects of technological advances and inactive recreational pursuits. You need to blend proper eating habits with vigorous exercise to develop and maintain a healthy functioning body.

Obesity and inactivity have been correlated with coronary heart disease, high blood pressure, diabetes, and other degenerative disorders. But obesity and overfatness are virtually unknown among vigorous, active people. Athletes, fitness enthusiasts, and active recreation-minded people seldom have excess body fat. Almost everyone is concerned about their body fat and their appearance, and many people go on diets when they become overfat. However, research has shown convincingly that special restrictive diets do not work over the long haul. Rather eating better and exercising more, combined with an overall commitment to live better, do work. The goal is not merely to lose fat but to keep it off, or better still, to never put it on. Now is the time to establish sound nutritional and exercise habits. Don't wait until your health and fitness have deteriorated.

Controlling body composition is about understanding energy balance. If a person wants to lose one pound of fat mass, they need to achieve a negative energy balance of 3,500 calories per week. Combining moderate dietary restriction with exercise is an effective long-term strategy for decreasing fat mass. Conversely, to gain weight, caloric consumption must exceed expenditure thereby creating a positive energy balance. Consuming 300 to 500 extra calories per day, primarily in the form of carbohydrates, will support a rate of weight gain that increases muscle mass and minimizes fat gain.

10 Putting It Together: Making Exercise a Way of Life

So here we are at the end of the road (or pool or workout room or…). Throughout this book we have attempted to make principles and guidelines for developing physical fitness as clear as possible. You now know there are no gimmicks or shortcuts to first improving and then maintaining lifelong physical fitness. Keeping that information in mind this final chapter offers tips on how to create a meaningful and easy-to-follow routine for whichever activity you choose and at whichever point in life you find yourself. This chapter attempts to complete the template for personalizing your workout design. Samples of simple forms for recording your progress and setting training goals are included in the Appendix.

Read the following questions and after each one formulate the answer in your mind. If you don't know the answer, then read the chapter with the intent of finding the answer. If you did answer the question, then read to make sure your answer is correct and not a misconception you have about how to put the book's information to work for you.

- How do you go about prioritizing your fitness goals?
- Why keep track of what you do during each workout?
- How can you fit your workouts into your day/week?
- How do you deal with exercising during vacations or holidays?
- Where can you turn to if you have questions or concerns about exercise?

HOW DO I PRIORITIZE MY FITNESS GOALS?

As we have discussed, the best place to start your fitness program is to define your fitness goals. Once your have defined your goals you need to come up with a time frame within which to accomplish them. Not everything has to be done today. List your goals in order of priority. Then consider a timeline for each goal, keeping your priorities in mind as you do so. This act of prioritizing makes a project that at first may feel overwhelming fit into very doable parts. Think 'short-term goals' and 'long-term goals'. An example of a short-term goal may be 'This first month I will walk for 30 minutes 3 days a week'. A long-term goal may be 'I will compete in a triathlon one year from today'. It helps if you also include intermediate goals along the way such as 'In 3 months exercise will play a regular, non-negotiable role in my life' or 'I will lose 15 pounds of body fat in 6 months'. Use the form found in Appendix D as an aid in planning these short- and long-term goals.

WHY IS KEEPING TRACK OF MY PROGRESS A GOOD IDEA?

For anyone who has ever embarked on a physical fitness program and stuck with it for any length of time, it's always a thrill to look back to your start and see how far you have come. Tracking your progress on paper can be uplifting as well as revealing since numbers don't lie. If you keep records of your progress they can be used to bolster your motivation if you fall into a stagnant period when you hit a plateau. Record-keeping is particularly important as you familiarize yourself with a new activity. Along with revealing any progress you are making, records can also point out flaws in your program that may be preventing you from moving to the next level of fitness.

Even if you don't like to keep records, realize that it is practically mandatory to do so when starting a new activity. You just can't rely on your head to keep track of time, miles, weight, reps and sets, active days and rest days. You may not have to write things down forever, especially if and when you find yourself on a maintenance program. Until that time, however, you will find records imperative. One exception is when you are working on equipment that stores your data for you. Since the vast majority of exercisers do not yet have access to this technology a simple exercise file should be kept in your workout bag for quick reference.

A favorite tool for tracking your cardiorespiratory endurance exercise program is a desk calendar. Since it holds an entire year's worth of workouts, you may be amazed (and amused) when you flip through and see how far you have come. Under each day there is usually enough space to write your activity's distance and duration along with your heart rate. If there is space, rate your workout or note unusual things along the way like weather or people you passed. Also available are commercial exercise logbooks that guide you through questions and comments to consider during your workout. An example of important data to record during an aerobic workout can be found on the example forms shown in Chapter 6 or in Appendix B.

Your resistance training log will be quite different since you are tracking items such as the muscle group being worked, the exercise used for that muscle group, how much weight you are lifting, and how many sets and repetitions you are performing. It may also be important to note seat and pad adjustments when using machine weights. An actual chart will be more helpful than a desk calendar since there is so much data to consider. It is helpful when your form groups your exercises by regions of the body, opposing muscle groups, and/or the order in which you typically perform them. Use these weight records during a workout to note such things as whether you need to advance to a heavier weight your next workout or whether a certain movement bothered your joints. Note anything and everything of importance that will help you do the right thing during your next workout. An example of a resistance training log can be found in Appendix C.

Tracking your body weight on a scale certainly does not tell the whole story when it comes to body composition. Remember, scales don't tell you how much fat or how much lean tissue makes up your body. However, if you have had some type of body composition assessment performed at the start of your fitness program and were given a body weight to strive for before being re-assessed, it is a good idea to regularly weigh and record that weight. Not long ago, fitness professionals recommended weighing only once weekly due in part to the slow nature of losing body fat as well as for preventing an obsession of your scale weight. Recently we have learned that people who have lost significant amounts of weight and, more importantly, have maintained that weight loss typically weigh more often than once weekly. Weighing yourself more frequently offers you the chance to avoid any creeping weight gain by catching yourself if you start to lose focus. A simple index card taped to the wall near your scale can be your recording method. Included in our aerobic exercise log (Appendix B) is space for you to record your weight in the comments section.

HOW CAN I FIND THE TIME TO EXERCISE?

As you begin to progress in a fitness program the resulting good feelings and success will help you to stay motivated. However, studies have shown that staying with a regular exercise program is not always as promising as we would like to think. It is imperative you make a firm pledge to stay with your exercise program, particularly during the early stages of establishing your new habit. It generally takes at least three to four months for most people to fully begin to appreciate the pleasures of stimulating exercise. This is when you reach the point where you are working out not because you have to, but because you want to.

As you design your workouts to eventually include all of the five fitness components you may wonder how much time this new lifestyle will require. Taking into account the recommended frequency and duration for each component, here is a 'time tally':

Cardiorespiratory endurance (aerobic exercise): 3 to 5 days for 20 to 60 minutes
Weekly Time Range: 100 to 180 minutes
Body composition (aerobic exercise): 5 to 7 days for 45+ minutes
Weekly Time Range: 225 to 315 minutes
**Choose EITHER cardiorespiratory endurance or body composition exercise, not both (since both involve aerobic activities).
Muscular strength and endurance: 2 to 3 days for approximately 60 minutes
Weekly Time Range: 120 to 180 minutes
Flexibility: daily for approximately 5 minutes
Weekly Time Range: 35 minutes

Taking the least possible combination of minutes we would possibly allot to exercise (100+120+35) and the most (315+180+35) we would arrive at the TOTAL WEEKLY TIME RANGE: 255 to 530 minutes. There are 10,080 minutes in a week. In terms of percentages, your workouts would take up 3 to 5% of your week. Does that sound extravagant? Does that sound impossible in a busy, hectic life? Or does 3 to 5% of your week sound very doable? We thought so.

Remember, there is no right or wrong time to exercise. The best time for you is the time when you have the energy and the opportunity to work out. We suggest you at least try exercising first thing in the morning since that routine eliminates the possibility for planned or unplanned events to get in your way. Another tip is to break up your workouts into more manageable chunks of time. If your goal is cardiorespiratory endurance, you can use three 10 minute segments spread throughout the day if you do not have a 30 minute chunk of time for aerobic exercise. Those segments can be timed

to precede your meals or can be used as energizing breaks throughout the day if you find yourself stuck at a desk. It may take as much as one year of experimenting with your variables, your goals, your personality, your energy ebbs and flows, and your lifestyle, before your routine is set.

A frequent complaint of would-be exercisers is that they don't have enough time to both exercise AND spend quality time with family, friends, or co-workers. Why not kill two birds with one stone by including another person or persons in your workout? It is well established that working out with others provides a stimulus to keep you going. This not only adds a social time for you and people important in your life but also tends to help you stay committed. No one wants to let a friend down by not showing up to a planned joint workout. If your time crunch has more to do with meeting new people, consider the opportunity YMCAs, university and college recreation centers, community centers, and private and corporate fitness centers provide to meet other fitness enthusiasts.

HOW DO I DEAL WITH VACATIONS OR HOLIDAYS?

People who are new to a fitness lifestyle may wonder how they will manage to maintain their workouts when holidays or vacations enter the picture. The simple answer is that neither should interfere with the other. In fact, exercising can actually enhance special events. Stressful holidays can be made much less so when you use vigorous exercise as a tension release. Time spent outdoors can clear your head and give you some perspective on your celebration.

Of course holiday celebrations tend to be loaded with eating and drinking (that's one reason they are called 'celebrations'). If you don't want to miss out on the goodies, pay for the privilege. This means expending a substantial amount of energy through exercise, particularly the day of and the day after a holiday get-together.

The combination of holidays and fitness is a great excuse for starting traditions. It might mean a New Year's Renewal Run followed by a healthy meal to kick off your resolutions. It might mean a Christmas Eve midnight cross-country ski outing or a Fourth of July open-water swim. It might mean a Labor Day End-of-Summer bike ride where everyone invites one person they met that summer to join the group. Don't be surprised if you and your friends vow to 'do this again next year!'.

Exercise and travel make great partners. If you are on vacation, what better way to see new sights and cities than to plan your bike rides, walks, or hikes around your new destination? Hotel concierges frequently direct runners to recommended routes out and back from the hotel. If you have a membership at a fitness center that is part of a national chain , you may have reciprocal rights to workout at any of their locations across the country. On a road trip, it might be as simple as practicing flexibility stretches when you take your hourly rest stop breaks.

Consider planning your vacation with an active itinerary built in. For instance, you could sea kayak with an outfitter, attend golf or tennis school, bike through a foreign country. If you have chosen a new fitness activity for your workout, one of your long-term goals may be a vacation that revolves around that activity. For instance, if you are currently learning to swim you could celebrate your newfound competence in the water by going on a snorkeling trip.

A key to staying with your routine during holidays or vacations is to strive to maintain your current fitness level, not increase it. If you are feeling overwhelmed by the additional demands on your time, perform your activity for the minimum suggested frequency and duration while maintaining your current intensity level. With a little creative management, fitness can find a place in the inevitable twists and turns of our lives. To coin a phrase, just do it.

WHERE CAN I GO TO GET HELP WITH MY EXERCISE PROGRAM?

From a professional standpoint it is exciting how frequently things change in the field of physical fitness and exercise science. From the participant's standpoint, however, it can be downright frustrating trying to keep up. The components and principles that we discuss in this book are based on many years of research applied to people of all fitness levels. This information, however, is always open to modifications as new research appears.

So where do you go to stay on top of new physical fitness trends and guidelines? Where do you go for answers to your fitness questions as your workout evolves and new goals enter the picture? Magazines geared to your fitness activity typically do a fine job discussing the latest trends. Articles on new equipment or new group exercise classes can excite and motivate you to either start or continue your exercise program. Just be aware that some of the information may be based on anecdotal evidence and/or trends endorsed by suppliers of products advertised in that magazine. For more objective (although maybe less glamorous) information on guidelines, we recommend any of the professional sources listed in Table 10.1. These sources provide scientifically grounded information that in turn can be trusted. Do not get frustrated if something in the exercise arena that you learned years ago has been debunked as a myth or has been tweaked somewhat. Just know that the exercise scientists performing the research are simply collecting more and more data in order to make our workouts safer, more effective, and inevitably more enjoyable.

Table 10.1. Good Sources For Information Regarding Exercise

American Council on Exercise (ACE) acefitness.org
American College of Sports Medicine (ACSM) acsm.org
National Strength and Conditioning Association (NSCA) nsca-lift.org

SUMMARY

This book has been written for you based on our knowledge and our experience of observing people who have become physically active regardless of their past exercise or athletic experiences. Do you personally recall physical education or athletic experiences when you were punished with exercise? Do you recall being embarrassed as you were made to feel physically inept? How ridiculous! No wonder so many people of all ages today are lacking in physical fitness and athletic skills. Optimizing your level of physical fitness does not include surviving punishing, exhaustive workouts, but rather exercising well within your present physical capacity.

Whatever you do, live a fitness lifestyle as if it were no big deal. In other words, once exercise and healthy eating become routine they should just naturally fit into your day without becoming a burden or another task you need to obsess over. Exercise as if your life depended on it, because in reality it does. Stay active and exercise regularly. Enjoy how physical activity makes you feel both during your workouts as well as afterward when you realize the gift you just gave yourself. Over the years, the rewards will get sweeter as fitness becomes YOUR way of life.

Appendix A

Directions for using the Personal Physical Fitness Progress Chart:

1. Record the date and results of your first (i.e. baseline) measurements in the left-most column. This is all you need to do the first time you test yourself and use the chart.
2. Whenever you reassess your fitness level write the date in a gray shaded box at the top of the chart.
3. Subtract your baseline measurement from the new test measure.
4. Plot the difference on the grid in the center of the column as shown in Figure 3.12.

For example, in Figure 3.12 the date of the first testing (i.e. baseline measure) was January 1 and the results of the chest press and body composition tests were 150 pounds and 28%, respectively. Retests were performed on February 13, March 31, and May 15. On the most recent retest dated May 15, the person bench pressed 175 pounds. The difference between 175 and the baseline measure of 150 was 25 pounds and thus plotted on the grid. Body composition on May 15 was determined to be 18%. Subtracting 28% from 18% yields a difference of -10%. In other words, percent body fat decreased by 10%. As a result. a dot was place in the column at -10.

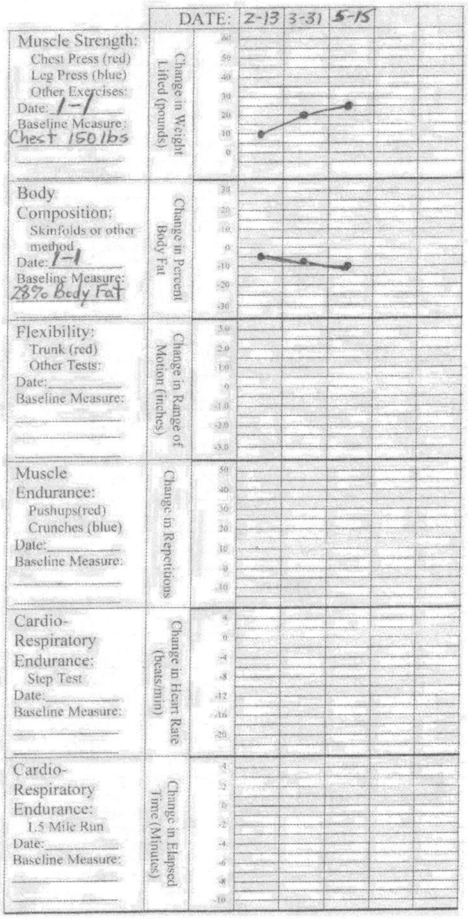

Figure 3.12: Sample Progression Chart

Appendix A

Personal Physical Fitness Progress Chart

See Chapter 3, Figure 3.12 for example of how to plot.

	DATE:													

Muscle Strength:
  Chest Press (red)
  Leg Press (blue)
  Other Exercises:
Date:_____
Baseline Measure:
_____
_____
_____

Change in Weight Lifted (pounds): 50, 45, 40, 35, 30, 25, 20, 15, 10, 5, 0, -5, -10

Body Composition:
  Skinfolds or other method
Date:_____
Baseline Measure:
_____
_____

Change in Percent Body Fat: 30, 25, 20, 15, 10, 5, 0, -5, -10, -15, -20, -25, -30

Flexibility:
  Trunk (red)
  Other Tests:
Date:_____
Baseline Measure:
_____
_____
_____

Change in Range of Motion (inches): 3.0, 2.5, 2.0, 1.5, 1.0, 0.5, 0, -0.5, -1.0, -1.5, -2.0, -2.5, -3.0

Muscle Endurance:
  Pushups(red)
  Crunches (blue)
Date:_____
Baseline Measure:
_____
_____

Change in Repetitions: 40, 35, 30, 25, 20, 15, 10, 5, 0, -5, -10, -15, -20

Cardio-Respiratory Endurance:
  Step Test
Date:_____
Baseline Measure:
_____
_____

Change in Heart Rate (beats/min): 4, 2, 0, -2, -4, -6, -8, -10, -12, -14, -16, -18, -20

Cardio-Respiratory Endurance:
  1.5 Mile Run
Date:_____
Baseline Measure:
_____
_____

Change in Elapsed Time (Minutes): 2, 1, 0, -1, -2, -3, -4, -5, -6, -7, -8, -9, -10

Appendix B

AEROBIC EXERCISE LOG

DATE	TIME OF DAY	MODE OF EXERCISE	DURATION / MILEAGE	TARGET HEART RATE RANGE	HEART RATE	
					MID	END

COMMENTS:

DATE	TIME OF DAY	MODE OF EXERCISE	DURATION / MILEAGE	TARGET HEART RATE RANGE	HEART RATE	
					MID	END

COMMENTS:

DATE	TIME OF DAY	MODE OF EXERCISE	DURATION / MILEAGE	TARGET HEART RATE RANGE	HEART RATE	
					MID	END

COMMENTS:

DATE	TIME OF DAY	MODE OF EXERCISE	DURATION / MILEAGE	TARGET HEART RATE RANGE	HEART RATE	
					MID	END

COMMENTS:

DATE	TIME OF DAY	MODE OF EXERCISE	DURATION / MILEAGE	TARGET HEART RATE RANGE	HEART RATE	
					MID	END

COMMENTS:

DATE	TIME OF DAY	MODE OF EXERCISE	DURATION / MILEAGE	TARGET HEART RATE RANGE	HEART RATE	
					MID	END

COMMENTS:

DATE	TIME OF DAY	MODE OF EXERCISE	DURATION / MILEAGE	TARGET HEART RATE RANGE	HEART RATE	
					MID	END

COMMENTS:

DATE	TIME OF DAY	MODE OF EXERCISE	DURATION / MILEAGE	TARGET HEART RATE RANGE	HEART RATE	
					MID	END

COMMENTS:

Appendix B

AEROBIC EXERCISE LOG

DATE	TIME OF DAY	MODE OF EXERCISE	DURATION / MILEAGE	TARGET HEART RATE RANGE	HEART RATE MID	END
COMMENTS:						
DATE	TIME OF DAY	MODE OF EXERCISE	DURATION / MILEAGE	TARGET HEART RATE RANGE	HEART RATE MID	END
COMMENTS:						
DATE	TIME OF DAY	MODE OF EXERCISE	DURATION / MILEAGE	TARGET HEART RATE RANGE	HEART RATE MID	END
COMMENTS:						
DATE	TIME OF DAY	MODE OF EXERCISE	DURATION / MILEAGE	TARGET HEART RATE RANGE	HEART RATE MID	END
COMMENTS:						
DATE	TIME OF DAY	MODE OF EXERCISE	DURATION / MILEAGE	TARGET HEART RATE RANGE	HEART RATE MID	END
COMMENTS:						
DATE	TIME OF DAY	MODE OF EXERCISE	DURATION / MILEAGE	TARGET HEART RATE RANGE	HEART RATE MID	END
COMMENTS:						
DATE	TIME OF DAY	MODE OF EXERCISE	DURATION / MILEAGE	TARGET HEART RATE RANGE	HEART RATE MID	END
COMMENTS:						
DATE	TIME OF DAY	MODE OF EXERCISE	DURATION / MILEAGE	TARGET HEART RATE RANGE	HEART RATE MID	END
COMMENTS:						

Appendix B

AEROBIC EXERCISE LOG

DATE	TIME OF DAY	MODE OF EXERCISE	DURATION / MILEAGE	TARGET HEART RATE RANGE	HEART RATE	
					MID	END
COMMENTS:						
DATE	TIME OF DAY	MODE OF EXERCISE	DURATION / MILEAGE	TARGET HEART RATE RANGE	HEART RATE	
					MID	END
COMMENTS:						
DATE	TIME OF DAY	MODE OF EXERCISE	DURATION / MILEAGE	TARGET HEART RATE RANGE	HEART RATE	
					MID	END
COMMENTS:						
DATE	TIME OF DAY	MODE OF EXERCISE	DURATION / MILEAGE	TARGET HEART RATE RANGE	HEART RATE	
					MID	END
COMMENTS:						
DATE	TIME OF DAY	MODE OF EXERCISE	DURATION / MILEAGE	TARGET HEART RATE RANGE	HEART RATE	
					MID	END
COMMENTS:						
DATE	TIME OF DAY	MODE OF EXERCISE	DURATION / MILEAGE	TARGET HEART RATE RANGE	HEART RATE	
					MID	END
COMMENTS:						
DATE	TIME OF DAY	MODE OF EXERCISE	DURATION / MILEAGE	TARGET HEART RATE RANGE	HEART RATE	
					MID	END
COMMENTS:						
DATE	TIME OF DAY	MODE OF EXERCISE	DURATION / MILEAGE	TARGET HEART RATE RANGE	HEART RATE	
					MID	END
COMMENTS:						

Appendix B

AEROBIC EXERCISE LOG

DATE	TIME OF DAY	MODE OF EXERCISE	DURATION / MILEAGE	TARGET HEART RATE RANGE	HEART RATE	
					MID	END

COMMENTS:

DATE	TIME OF DAY	MODE OF EXERCISE	DURATION / MILEAGE	TARGET HEART RATE RANGE	HEART RATE	
					MID	END

COMMENTS:

DATE	TIME OF DAY	MODE OF EXERCISE	DURATION / MILEAGE	TARGET HEART RATE RANGE	HEART RATE	
					MID	END

COMMENTS:

DATE	TIME OF DAY	MODE OF EXERCISE	DURATION / MILEAGE	TARGET HEART RATE RANGE	HEART RATE	
					MID	END

COMMENTS:

DATE	TIME OF DAY	MODE OF EXERCISE	DURATION / MILEAGE	TARGET HEART RATE RANGE	HEART RATE	
					MID	END

COMMENTS:

DATE	TIME OF DAY	MODE OF EXERCISE	DURATION / MILEAGE	TARGET HEART RATE RANGE	HEART RATE	
					MID	END

COMMENTS:

DATE	TIME OF DAY	MODE OF EXERCISE	DURATION / MILEAGE	TARGET HEART RATE RANGE	HEART RATE	
					MID	END

COMMENTS:

DATE	TIME OF DAY	MODE OF EXERCISE	DURATION / MILEAGE	TARGET HEART RATE RANGE	HEART RATE	
					MID	END

COMMENTS:

Appendix B

AEROBIC EXERCISE LOG

DATE	TIME OF DAY	MODE OF EXERCISE	DURATION / MILEAGE	TARGET HEART RATE RANGE	HEART RATE	
					MID	END

COMMENTS:

DATE	TIME OF DAY	MODE OF EXERCISE	DURATION / MILEAGE	TARGET HEART RATE RANGE	HEART RATE	
					MID	END

COMMENTS:

DATE	TIME OF DAY	MODE OF EXERCISE	DURATION / MILEAGE	TARGET HEART RATE RANGE	HEART RATE	
					MID	END

COMMENTS:

DATE	TIME OF DAY	MODE OF EXERCISE	DURATION / MILEAGE	TARGET HEART RATE RANGE	HEART RATE	
					MID	END

COMMENTS:

DATE	TIME OF DAY	MODE OF EXERCISE	DURATION / MILEAGE	TARGET HEART RATE RANGE	HEART RATE	
					MID	END

COMMENTS:

DATE	TIME OF DAY	MODE OF EXERCISE	DURATION / MILEAGE	TARGET HEART RATE RANGE	HEART RATE	
					MID	END

COMMENTS:

DATE	TIME OF DAY	MODE OF EXERCISE	DURATION / MILEAGE	TARGET HEART RATE RANGE	HEART RATE	
					MID	END

COMMENTS:

DATE	TIME OF DAY	MODE OF EXERCISE	DURATION / MILEAGE	TARGET HEART RATE RANGE	HEART RATE	
					MID	END

COMMENTS:

Appendix B

AEROBIC EXERCISE LOG

DATE	TIME OF DAY	MODE OF EXERCISE	DURATION / MILEAGE	TARGET HEART RATE RANGE	HEART RATE	
					MID	END
COMMENTS:						
DATE	TIME OF DAY	MODE OF EXERCISE	DURATION / MILEAGE	TARGET HEART RATE RANGE	HEART RATE	
					MID	END
COMMENTS:						
DATE	TIME OF DAY	MODE OF EXERCISE	DURATION / MILEAGE	TARGET HEART RATE RANGE	HEART RATE	
					MID	END
COMMENTS:						
DATE	TIME OF DAY	MODE OF EXERCISE	DURATION / MILEAGE	TARGET HEART RATE RANGE	HEART RATE	
					MID	END
COMMENTS:						
DATE	TIME OF DAY	MODE OF EXERCISE	DURATION / MILEAGE	TARGET HEART RATE RANGE	HEART RATE	
					MID	END
COMMENTS:						
DATE	TIME OF DAY	MODE OF EXERCISE	DURATION / MILEAGE	TARGET HEART RATE RANGE	HEART RATE	
					MID	END
COMMENTS:						
DATE	TIME OF DAY	MODE OF EXERCISE	DURATION / MILEAGE	TARGET HEART RATE RANGE	HEART RATE	
					MID	END
COMMENTS:						
DATE	TIME OF DAY	MODE OF EXERCISE	DURATION / MILEAGE	TARGET HEART RATE RANGE	HEART RATE	
					MID	END
COMMENTS:						

Appendix B

AEROBIC EXERCISE LOG

DATE	TIME OF DAY	MODE OF EXERCISE	DURATION / MILEAGE	TARGET HEART RATE RANGE	HEART RATE	
					MID	END

COMMENTS:

DATE	TIME OF DAY	MODE OF EXERCISE	DURATION / MILEAGE	TARGET HEART RATE RANGE	HEART RATE	
					MID	END

COMMENTS:

DATE	TIME OF DAY	MODE OF EXERCISE	DURATION / MILEAGE	TARGET HEART RATE RANGE	HEART RATE	
					MID	END

COMMENTS:

DATE	TIME OF DAY	MODE OF EXERCISE	DURATION / MILEAGE	TARGET HEART RATE RANGE	HEART RATE	
					MID	END

COMMENTS:

DATE	TIME OF DAY	MODE OF EXERCISE	DURATION / MILEAGE	TARGET HEART RATE RANGE	HEART RATE	
					MID	END

COMMENTS:

DATE	TIME OF DAY	MODE OF EXERCISE	DURATION / MILEAGE	TARGET HEART RATE RANGE	HEART RATE	
					MID	END

COMMENTS:

DATE	TIME OF DAY	MODE OF EXERCISE	DURATION / MILEAGE	TARGET HEART RATE RANGE	HEART RATE	
					MID	END

COMMENTS:

DATE	TIME OF DAY	MODE OF EXERCISE	DURATION / MILEAGE	TARGET HEART RATE RANGE	HEART RATE	
					MID	END

COMMENTS:

Appendix B

AEROBIC EXERCISE LOG

DATE	TIME OF DAY	MODE OF EXERCISE	DURATION / MILEAGE	TARGET HEART RATE RANGE	HEART RATE	
					MID	END

COMMENTS:

DATE	TIME OF DAY	MODE OF EXERCISE	DURATION / MILEAGE	TARGET HEART RATE RANGE	HEART RATE	
					MID	END

COMMENTS:

DATE	TIME OF DAY	MODE OF EXERCISE	DURATION / MILEAGE	TARGET HEART RATE RANGE	HEART RATE	
					MID	END

COMMENTS:

DATE	TIME OF DAY	MODE OF EXERCISE	DURATION / MILEAGE	TARGET HEART RATE RANGE	HEART RATE	
					MID	END

COMMENTS:

DATE	TIME OF DAY	MODE OF EXERCISE	DURATION / MILEAGE	TARGET HEART RATE RANGE	HEART RATE	
					MID	END

COMMENTS:

DATE	TIME OF DAY	MODE OF EXERCISE	DURATION / MILEAGE	TARGET HEART RATE RANGE	HEART RATE	
					MID	END

COMMENTS:

DATE	TIME OF DAY	MODE OF EXERCISE	DURATION / MILEAGE	TARGET HEART RATE RANGE	HEART RATE	
					MID	END

COMMENTS:

DATE	TIME OF DAY	MODE OF EXERCISE	DURATION / MILEAGE	TARGET HEART RATE RANGE	HEART RATE	
					MID	END

COMMENTS:

Appendix B

AEROBIC EXERCISE LOG

DATE	TIME OF DAY	MODE OF EXERCISE	DURATION / MILEAGE	TARGET HEART RATE RANGE	HEART RATE	
					MID	END

COMMENTS:

DATE	TIME OF DAY	MODE OF EXERCISE	DURATION / MILEAGE	TARGET HEART RATE RANGE	HEART RATE	
					MID	END

COMMENTS:

DATE	TIME OF DAY	MODE OF EXERCISE	DURATION / MILEAGE	TARGET HEART RATE RANGE	HEART RATE	
					MID	END

COMMENTS:

DATE	TIME OF DAY	MODE OF EXERCISE	DURATION / MILEAGE	TARGET HEART RATE RANGE	HEART RATE	
					MID	END

COMMENTS:

DATE	TIME OF DAY	MODE OF EXERCISE	DURATION / MILEAGE	TARGET HEART RATE RANGE	HEART RATE	
					MID	END

COMMENTS:

DATE	TIME OF DAY	MODE OF EXERCISE	DURATION / MILEAGE	TARGET HEART RATE RANGE	HEART RATE	
					MID	END

COMMENTS:

DATE	TIME OF DAY	MODE OF EXERCISE	DURATION / MILEAGE	TARGET HEART RATE RANGE	HEART RATE	
					MID	END

COMMENTS:

DATE	TIME OF DAY	MODE OF EXERCISE	DURATION / MILEAGE	TARGET HEART RATE RANGE	HEART RATE	
					MID	END

COMMENTS:

Appendix C

RESISTANCE TRAINING LOG

BODY REGION & EXERCISE USED		WORKOUT #1 Date: _____			WORKOUT #2 Date: _____			WORKOUT #3 Date: _____		
		SET 1	SET 2	SET 3	SET 1	SET 2	SET 3	SET 1	SET 2	SET 3
1: Hips & Front of Thighs	Weight / Reps									
	Comments									
2: Back of Thighs	Weight / Reps									
	Comments									
3: Chest	Weight / Reps									
	Comments									
4: Upper Back	Weight / Reps									
	Comments									
5: Shoulders	Weight / Reps									
	Comments									
6: Lower Back	Weight / Reps									
	Comments									
7: Abdominals	Weight / Reps									
	Comments									
8: Side of Trunk	Weight / Reps									
	Comments									
9: Front of Upper Arms	Weight / Reps									
	Comments									
10: Back of Upper Arms	Weight / Reps									
	Comments									
11: Front of Lower Leg	Weight / Reps									
	Comments									
12: Back of Lower Leg	Weight / Reps									
	Comments									

Appendix C

RESISTANCE TRAINING LOG

BODY REGION & EXERCISE USED		WORKOUT #1 Date: _____			WORKOUT #2 Date: _____			WORKOUT #3 Date: _____		
		SET 1	SET 2	SET 3	SET 1	SET 2	SET 3	SET 1	SET 2	SET 3
1: Hips & Front of Thighs	Weight / Reps									
	Comments									
2: Back of Thighs	Weight / Reps									
	Comments									
3: Chest	Weight / Reps									
	Comments									
4: Upper Back	Weight / Reps									
	Comments									
5: Shoulders	Weight / Reps									
	Comments									
6: Lower Back	Weight / Reps									
	Comments									
7: Abdominals	Weight / Reps									
	Comments									
8: Side of Trunk	Weight / Reps									
	Comments									
9: Front of Upper Arms	Weight / Reps									
	Comments									
10: Back of Upper Arms	Weight / Reps									
	Comments									
11: Front of Lower Leg	Weight / Reps									
	Comments									
12: Back of Lower Leg	Weight / Reps									
	Comments									

Appendix C

RESISTANCE TRAINING LOG

BODY REGION & EXERCISE USED		WORKOUT #1 Date: ___			WORKOUT #2 Date: ___			WORKOUT #3 Date: ___		
		SET 1	SET 2	SET 3	SET 1	SET 2	SET 3	SET 1	SET 2	SET 3
1: Hips & Front of Thighs	Weight / Reps									
	Comments									
2: Back of Thighs	Weight / Reps									
	Comments									
3: Chest	Weight / Reps									
	Comments									
4: Upper Back	Weight / Reps									
	Comments									
5: Shoulders	Weight / Reps									
	Comments									
6: Lower Back	Weight / Reps									
	Comments									
7: Abdominals	Weight / Reps									
	Comments									
8: Side of Trunk	Weight / Reps									
	Comments									
9: Front of Upper Arms	Weight / Reps									
	Comments									
10: Back of Upper Arms	Weight / Reps									
	Comments									
11: Front of Lower Leg	Weight / Reps									
	Comments									
12: Back of Lower Leg	Weight / Reps									
	Comments									

Appendix C

RESISTANCE TRAINING LOG

BODY REGION & EXERCISE USED		WORKOUT #1 Date: _____			WORKOUT #2 Date: _____			WORKOUT #3 Date: _____		
		SET 1	SET 2	SET 3	SET 1	SET 2	SET 3	SET 1	SET 2	SET 3
1: Hips & Front of Thighs	Weight / Reps									
	Comments									
2: Back of Thighs	Weight / Reps									
	Comments									
3: Chest	Weight / Reps									
	Comments									
4: Upper Back	Weight / Reps									
	Comments									
5: Shoulders	Weight / Reps									
	Comments									
6: Lower Back	Weight / Reps									
	Comments									
7: Abdominals	Weight / Reps									
	Comments									
8: Side of Trunk	Weight / Reps									
	Comments									
9: Front of Upper Arms	Weight / Reps									
	Comments									
10: Back of Upper Arms	Weight / Reps									
	Comments									
11: Front of Lower Leg	Weight / Reps									
	Comments									
12: Back of Lower Leg	Weight / Reps									
	Comments									

Appendix C

RESISTANCE TRAINING LOG

BODY REGION & EXERCISE USED		WORKOUT #1 Date: _____			WORKOUT #2 Date: _____			WORKOUT #3 Date: _____		
		SET 1	SET 2	SET 3	SET 1	SET 2	SET 3	SET 1	SET 2	SET 3
1: Hips & Front of Thighs	Weight / Reps									
	Comments									
2: Back of Thighs	Weight / Reps									
	Comments									
3: Chest	Weight / Reps									
	Comments									
4: Upper Back	Weight / Reps									
	Comments									
5: Shoulders	Weight / Reps									
	Comments									
6: Lower Back	Weight / Reps									
	Comments									
7: Abdominals	Weight / Reps									
	Comments									
8: Side of Trunk	Weight / Reps									
	Comments									
9: Front of Upper Arms	Weight / Reps									
	Comments									
10: Back of Upper Arms	Weight / Reps									
	Comments									
11: Front of Lower Leg	Weight / Reps									
	Comments									
12: Back of Lower Leg	Weight / Reps									
	Comments									

Appendix C

RESISTANCE TRAINING LOG

BODY REGION & EXERCISE USED		WORKOUT #1 Date: _____			WORKOUT #2 Date: _____			WORKOUT #3 Date: _____		
		SET 1	SET 2	SET 3	SET 1	SET 2	SET 3	SET 1	SET 2	SET 3
1: Hips & Front of Thighs	Weight / Reps									
	Comments									
2: Back of Thighs	Weight / Reps									
	Comments									
3: Chest	Weight / Reps									
	Comments									
4: Upper Back	Weight / Reps									
	Comments									
5: Shoulders	Weight / Reps									
	Comments									
6: Lower Back	Weight / Reps									
	Comments									
7: Abdominals	Weight / Reps									
	Comments									
8: Side of Trunk	Weight / Reps									
	Comments									
9: Front of Upper Arms	Weight / Reps									
	Comments									
10: Back of Upper Arms	Weight / Reps									
	Comments									
11: Front of Lower Leg	Weight / Reps									
	Comments									
12: Back of Lower Leg	Weight / Reps									
	Comments									

Appendix C

RESISTANCE TRAINING LOG

BODY REGION & EXERCISE USED		WORKOUT #1 Date: _____			WORKOUT #2 Date: _____			WORKOUT #3 Date: _____		
		SET 1	SET 2	SET 3	SET 1	SET 2	SET 3	SET 1	SET 2	SET 3
1: Hips & Front of Thighs	Weight / Reps									
	Comments									
2: Back of Thighs	Weight / Reps									
	Comments									
3: Chest	Weight / Reps									
	Comments									
4: Upper Back	Weight / Reps									
	Comments									
5: Shoulders	Weight / Reps									
	Comments									
6: Lower Back	Weight / Reps									
	Comments									
7: Abdominals	Weight / Reps									
	Comments									
8: Side of Trunk	Weight / Reps									
	Comments									
9: Front of Upper Arms	Weight / Reps									
	Comments									
10: Back of Upper Arms	Weight / Reps									
	Comments									
11: Front of Lower Leg	Weight / Reps									
	Comments									
12: Back of Lower Leg	Weight / Reps									
	Comments									

Appendix C

RESISTANCE TRAINING LOG

BODY REGION & EXERCISE USED		WORKOUT #1 Date: _____			WORKOUT #2 Date: _____			WORKOUT #3 Date: _____		
		SET 1	SET 2	SET 3	SET 1	SET 2	SET 3	SET 1	SET 2	SET 3
1: Hips & Front of Thighs	Weight/Reps									
	Comments									
2: Back of Thighs	Weight/Reps									
	Comments									
3: Chest	Weight/Reps									
	Comments									
4: Upper Back	Weight/Reps									
	Comments									
5: Shoulders	Weight/Reps									
	Comments									
6: Lower Back	Weight/Reps									
	Comments									
7: Abdominals	Weight/Reps									
	Comments									
8: Side of Trunk	Weight/Reps									
	Comments									
9: Front of Upper Arms	Weight/Reps									
	Comments									
10: Back of Upper Arms	Weight/Reps									
	Comments									
11: Front of Lower Leg	Weight/Reps									
	Comments									
12: Back of Lower Leg	Weight/Reps									
	Comments									

Appendix C

RESISTANCE TRAINING LOG

BODY REGION & EXERCISE USED		WORKOUT #1 Date: _____			WORKOUT #2 Date: _____			WORKOUT #3 Date: _____		
		SET 1	SET 2	SET 3	SET 1	SET 2	SET 3	SET 1	SET 2	SET 3
1: Hips & Front of Thighs	Weight / Reps									
	Comments									
2: Back of Thighs	Weight / Reps									
	Comments									
3: Chest	Weight / Reps									
	Comments									
4: Upper Back	Weight / Reps									
	Comments									
5: Shoulders	Weight / Reps									
	Comments									
6: Lower Back	Weight / Reps									
	Comments									
7: Abdominals	Weight / Reps									
	Comments									
8: Side of Trunk	Weight / Reps									
	Comments									
9: Front of Upper Arms	Weight / Reps									
	Comments									
10: Back of Upper Arms	Weight / Reps									
	Comments									
11: Front of Lower Leg	Weight / Reps									
	Comments									
12: Back of Lower Leg	Weight / Reps									
	Comments									

Appendix C

RESISTANCE TRAINING LOG

BODY REGION & EXERCISE USED		WORKOUT #1 Date: _____			WORKOUT #2 Date: _____			WORKOUT #3 Date: _____		
		SET 1	SET 2	SET 3	SET 1	SET 2	SET 3	SET 1	SET 2	SET 3
1: Hips & Front of Thighs	Weight / Reps									
	Comments									
2: Back of Thighs	Weight / Reps									
	Comments									
3: Chest	Weight / Reps									
	Comments									
4: Upper Back	Weight / Reps									
	Comments									
5: Shoulders	Weight / Reps									
	Comments									
6: Lower Back	Weight / Reps									
	Comments									
7: Abdominals	Weight / Reps									
	Comments									
8: Side of Trunk	Weight / Reps									
	Comments									
9: Front of Upper Arms	Weight / Reps									
	Comments									
10: Back of Upper Arms	Weight / Reps									
	Comments									
11: Front of Lower Leg	Weight / Reps									
	Comments									
12: Back of Lower Leg	Weight / Reps									
	Comments									

Appendix C

RESISTANCE TRAINING LOG

BODY REGION & EXERCISE USED		WORKOUT #1 Date: _____			WORKOUT #2 Date: _____			WORKOUT #3 Date: _____		
		SET 1	SET 2	SET 3	SET 1	SET 2	SET 3	SET 1	SET 2	SET 3
1: Hips & Front of Thighs	Weight / Reps									
	Comments									
2: Back of Thighs	Weight / Reps									
	Comments									
3: Chest	Weight / Reps									
	Comments									
4: Upper Back	Weight / Reps									
	Comments									
5: Shoulders	Weight / Reps									
	Comments									
6: Lower Back	Weight / Reps									
	Comments									
7: Abdominals	Weight / Reps									
	Comments									
8: Side of Trunk	Weight / Reps									
	Comments									
9: Front of Upper Arms	Weight / Reps									
	Comments									
10: Back of Upper Arms	Weight / Reps									
	Comments									
11: Front of Lower Leg	Weight / Reps									
	Comments									
12: Back of Lower Leg	Weight / Reps									
	Comments									

Appendix C

RESISTANCE TRAINING LOG

BODY REGION & EXERCISE USED		WORKOUT #1 Date: _____			WORKOUT #2 Date: _____			WORKOUT #3 Date: _____		
		SET 1	SET 2	SET 3	SET 1	SET 2	SET 3	SET 1	SET 2	SET 3
1: Hips & Front of Thighs	Weight / Reps									
	Comments									
2: Back of Thighs	Weight / Reps									
	Comments									
3: Chest	Weight / Reps									
	Comments									
4: Upper Back	Weight / Reps									
	Comments									
5: Shoulders	Weight / Reps									
	Comments									
6: Lower Back	Weight / Reps									
	Comments									
7: Abdominals	Weight / Reps									
	Comments									
8: Side of Trunk	Weight / Reps									
	Comments									
9: Front of Upper Arms	Weight / Reps									
	Comments									
10: Back of Upper Arms	Weight / Reps									
	Comments									
11: Front of Lower Leg	Weight / Reps									
	Comments									
12: Back of Lower Leg	Weight / Reps									
	Comments									

Appendix C

RESISTANCE TRAINING LOG

BODY REGION & EXERCISE USED		WORKOUT #1 Date: _____			WORKOUT #2 Date: _____			WORKOUT #3 Date: _____		
		SET 1	SET 2	SET 3	SET 1	SET 2	SET 3	SET 1	SET 2	SET 3
1: Hips & Front of Thighs	Weight / Reps									
	Comments									
2: Back of Thighs	Weight / Reps									
	Comments									
3: Chest	Weight / Reps									
	Comments									
4: Upper Back	Weight / Reps									
	Comments									
5: Shoulders	Weight / Reps									
	Comments									
6: Lower Back	Weight / Reps									
	Comments									
7: Abdominals	Weight / Reps									
	Comments									
8: Side of Trunk	Weight / Reps									
	Comments									
9: Front of Upper Arms	Weight / Reps									
	Comments									
10: Back of Upper Arms	Weight / Reps									
	Comments									
11: Front of Lower Leg	Weight / Reps									
	Comments									
12: Back of Lower Leg	Weight / Reps									
	Comments									

Appendix C

RESISTANCE TRAINING LOG

BODY REGION & EXERCISE USED		WORKOUT #1 Date: _____			WORKOUT #2 Date: _____			WORKOUT #3 Date: _____		
		SET 1	SET 2	SET 3	SET 1	SET 2	SET 3	SET 1	SET 2	SET 3
1: Hips & Front of Thighs	Weight / Reps									
	Comments									
2: Back of Thighs	Weight / Reps									
	Comments									
3: Chest	Weight / Reps									
	Comments									
4: Upper Back	Weight / Reps									
	Comments									
5: Shoulders	Weight / Reps									
	Comments									
6: Lower Back	Weight / Reps									
	Comments									
7: Abdominals	Weight / Reps									
	Comments									
8: Side of Trunk	Weight / Reps									
	Comments									
9: Front of Upper Arms	Weight / Reps									
	Comments									
10: Back of Upper Arms	Weight / Reps									
	Comments									
11: Front of Lower Leg	Weight / Reps									
	Comments									
12: Back of Lower Leg	Weight / Reps									
	Comments									

Appendix C

RESISTANCE TRAINING LOG

BODY REGION & EXERCISE USED		WORKOUT #1 Date: _____			WORKOUT #2 Date: _____			WORKOUT #3 Date: _____		
		SET 1	SET 2	SET 3	SET 1	SET 2	SET 3	SET 1	SET 2	SET 3
1: Hips & Front of Thighs	Weight / Reps									
	Comments									
2: Back of Thighs	Weight / Reps									
	Comments									
3: Chest	Weight / Reps									
	Comments									
4: Upper Back	Weight / Reps									
	Comments									
5: Shoulders	Weight / Reps									
	Comments									
6: Lower Back	Weight / Reps									
	Comments									
7: Abdominals	Weight / Reps									
	Comments									
8: Side of Trunk	Weight / Reps									
	Comments									
9: Front of Upper Arms	Weight / Reps									
	Comments									
10: Back of Upper Arms	Weight / Reps									
	Comments									
11: Front of Lower Leg	Weight / Reps									
	Comments									
12: Back of Lower Leg	Weight / Reps									
	Comments									

Appendix C

RESISTANCE TRAINING LOG

BODY REGION & EXERCISE USED		WORKOUT #1 Date: _____			WORKOUT #2 Date: _____			WORKOUT #3 Date: _____		
		SET 1	SET 2	SET 3	SET 1	SET 2	SET 3	SET 1	SET 2	SET 3
1: Hips & Front of Thighs	Weight / Reps									
	Comments									
2: Back of Thighs	Weight / Reps									
	Comments									
3: Chest	Weight / Reps									
	Comments									
4: Upper Back	Weight / Reps									
	Comments									
5: Shoulders	Weight / Reps									
	Comments									
6: Lower Back	Weight / Reps									
	Comments									
7: Abdominals	Weight / Reps									
	Comments									
8: Side of Trunk	Weight / Reps									
	Comments									
9: Front of Upper Arms	Weight / Reps									
	Comments									
10: Back of Upper Arms	Weight / Reps									
	Comments									
11: Front of Lower Leg	Weight / Reps									
	Comments									
12: Back of Lower Leg	Weight / Reps									
	Comments									

Appendix D

Short and Long-Term Fitness Goals

This Month	
Cardiorespiratory Endurance	
Body Composition	
Muscular Strength	
Muscular Endurance	
Flexibility	
Other	
One Month From Now	
Cardiorespiratory Endurance	
Body Composition	
Muscular Strength	
Muscular Endurance	
Flexibility	
Other	
Three Months From Now	
Cardiorespiratory Endurance	
Body Composition	
Muscular Strength	
Muscular Endurance	
Flexibility	
Other	
Six Months From Now	
Cardiorespiratory Endurance	
Body Composition	
Muscular Strength	
Muscular Endurance	
Flexibility	
Other	
One Year From Now	
Cardiorespiratory Endurance	
Body Composition	
Muscular Strength	
Muscular Endurance	
Flexibility	
Other	

Appendix E

Fitness Assessment Data Sheet

Name: _____ Date: _____

Age: _____ Height: _____ Weight: _____

Chest Press (in pounds)

Measure 1 _____ Measure 2 _____ Measure 3 _____ Best of 3 _____

Best measure divided by body weight _____ (1 RM/body weight)

Norm category _____

Leg Press (in pounds)

Measure 1 _____ Measure 2 _____ Measure 3 _____ Best of 3 _____

Best measure divided by body weight _____ (1 RM/body weight)

Norm category _____

Body Composition (skinfold measures in millimeters)

	Measure 1	Measure 2	Measure 3	Average of 3 Measures
Triceps	_____	_____	_____	_____
Subscapula	_____	_____	_____	_____
Midaxillary	_____	_____	_____	_____
Suprailiac	_____	_____	_____	_____
Abdomen	_____	_____	_____	_____
Thigh	_____	_____	_____	_____

Sum of 6 averages = _____

Percent body fat (see Figure 3.3) _____

Norm category _____

Trunk Flexion (in inches)

Measure 1 _____ Measure 2 _____ Measure 3 _____ Best of 3 _____

Norm category _____

Push-ups (repetitions)

Number of push-ups in 1 minute _____ Norm category _____

Abdominal Crunches (repetitions)

Number of abdominal crunches in 1 minute _____ Norm category _____

1.5-Mile Run (in minutes:seconds)

Time for 1.5 mile run _____ Norm category _____

Step Test (heart rate)

Recovery heart rate 1:00 to 1:30 _____

Recovery heart rate 2:00 to 2:30 _____

Recovery heart rate 3:00 to 3:30 _____

Sum of 3 recovery heart rates (recovery index) _____

Norm category _____

Appendix E

Fitness Assessment Data Sheet

Name: _____ Date: _____

Age: _____ Height: _____ Weight: _____

Chest Press (in pounds)

Measure 1 _____ Measure 2 _____ Measure 3 _____ Best of 3 _____

Best measure divided by body weight _____ (1 RM/body weight)

Norm category _____

Leg Press (in pounds)

Measure 1 _____ Measure 2 _____ Measure 3 _____ Best of 3 _____

Best measure divided by body weight _____ (1 RM/body weight)

Norm category _____

Body Composition (skinfold measures in millimeters)

	Measure 1	Measure 2	Measure 3	Average of 3 Measures
Triceps	_____	_____	_____	_____
Subscapula	_____	_____	_____	_____
Midaxillary	_____	_____	_____	_____
Suprailiac	_____	_____	_____	_____
Abdomen	_____	_____	_____	_____
Thigh	_____	_____	_____	_____
			Sum of 6 averages =	_____

Percent body fat (see Figure 3.3) _____

Norm category _____

Trunk Flexion (in inches)

Measure 1 _____ Measure 2 _____ Measure 3 _____ Best of 3 _____

Norm category _____

Push-ups (repetitions)

Number of push-ups in 1 minute _____ Norm category _____

Abdominal Crunches (repetitions)

Number of abdominal crunches in 1 minute _____ Norm category _____

1.5-Mile Run (in minutes:seconds)

Time for 1.5 mile run _____ Norm category _____

Step Test (heart rate)

Recovery heart rate 1:00 to 1:30 _____

Recovery heart rate 2:00 to 2:30 _____

Recovery heart rate 3:00 to 3:30 _____

Sum of 3 recovery heart rates (recovery index) _____

Norm category _____

Appendix E

Fitness Assessment Data Sheet

Name: _____ Date: _____

Age: _____ Height: _____ Weight: _____

Chest Press (in pounds)

Measure 1 _____ Measure 2 _____ Measure 3 _____ Best of 3 _____

Best measure divided by body weight _____ (1 RM/body weight)

Norm category _____

Leg Press (in pounds)

Measure 1 _____ Measure 2 _____ Measure 3 _____ Best of 3 _____

Best measure divided by body weight _____ (1 RM/body weight)

Norm category _____

Body Composition (skinfold measures in millimeters)

	Measure 1	Measure 2	Measure 3	Average of 3 Measures
Triceps	_____	_____	_____	_____
Subscapula	_____	_____	_____	_____
Midaxillary	_____	_____	_____	_____
Suprailiac	_____	_____	_____	_____
Abdomen	_____	_____	_____	_____
Thigh	_____	_____	_____	_____

Sum of 6 averages = _____

Percent body fat (see Figure 3.3) _____

Norm category _____

Trunk Flexion (in inches)

Measure 1 _____ Measure 2 _____ Measure 3 _____ Best of 3 _____

Norm category _____

Push-ups (repetitions)

Number of push-ups in 1 minute _____ Norm category _____

Abdominal Crunches (repetitions)

Number of abdominal crunches in 1 minute _____ Norm category _____

1.5-Mile Run (in minutes:seconds)

Time for 1.5 mile run _____ Norm category _____

Step Test (heart rate)

Recovery heart rate 1:00 to 1:30 _____

Recovery heart rate 2:00 to 2:30 _____

Recovery heart rate 3:00 to 3:30 _____

Sum of 3 recovery heart rates (recovery index) _____

Norm category _____

Index

training programs, male/female differences, 21–22
triathletes, cardiorespiratory endurance activities, 53
triceps
    skinfold caliper measurement, 28–29
    stretching, 101
trunk flexion, flexibility assessment, 30
trunk, resistance exercises, 90–91

U

underwater weighing, body composition assessment, 28
United States Centers for Disease Control, 3–4
unsaturated fats, 110
upper arms, resistance exercises, 91–93
upper back
    resistance exercises, 87–88
    stretching, 101, 102–103

V

vacations, exercise issues, 125–126
Valslva maneuver, 79
vitamins, 112

W

walking
    cardiorespiratory endurance activity, 53–54, 61–64
    weight-bearing exercise, 52
warm-up
    cardiorespiratory endurance training, 44–45
    flexibility training, 45
    reasons for, 43–44
    resistance training, 45, 81
    stretching misconceptions, 44
    workout element, 43–45
water aerobics, cardiorespiratory endurance training, 54, 68

water, intake importance, 113
water running, cardiorespiratory endurance training, 54, 68
Web sites
    ACE (American Council on Exercise), 126
    ACSM (American College of Sports Medicine), 126
    My Pyramid Food Plan, 114
    NCSA (National Strength and Conditioning Association), 126
weekend warriors, cardiorespiratory endurance training, 60
weight gain, nutrition guidelines, 120–121
weight lifter's blackout, 79
weight lifting
    muscle building, 14–15
    progressive resistance training, 20–21
    resistance exercise, 71
    spotters, 80
weight loss, cardiorespiratory endurance adjustments, 60–61
weight training, free weight/spotter, 25
weight-bearing exercise, 52
weights, resistance training guidelines, 77–78
wellness, 1-4
workouts
    conditioning period, 45–46
    cool-down, 46–47
    heart rate measurement, 57–58
    resistance training duration, 78
    speedplay, 58–59
    warm-up, 43–45
wrist/knee straps, resistance training, 81–82

Y

yoga plough, avoiding, 98